ICONIC HOTELS OF THE WORLD

CARSTEN K. RATH

ICONIC HOTELS

OF THE WORLD

A Journey through Luxury
and History

PRESTEL
Munich · London · New York

CONTENTS

A selection of the most important houses in the history of hospitality – global icons and role models over generations:

P
Kärntnerstraße
Tiefgarage
Zufahrt über Ring
Direkter Zugang
zur Staatsoper
ALBERTINA
AUTOBUS
HALTESTELLE

EUROPA

RECEP
140
141
143
144
236
240
241
243
244

93
94
95
96

INTRODUCTION

Be My Guest

It was trade routes in the ancient world that first gave rise to the need for guest accommodations. This was for travellers who moved with their precious cargos of spices, silks and other goods in horse- or camel-drawn caravans across Asia and the Middle East. A day's travel for such voyagers might have only been fifteen or twenty miles, and so caravanserai, or roadside inns, sprang up along specific highways and outside the gates of major towns and cities. These were places, often fortified and with an inner courtyard, where weary travellers could rest up safely, lodge their goods and stable their animals for a night or two. These simple inns provided in short the whole basis of our modern-day hotels. With the advent of Christianity and Islam, and the practices of both these faiths to undertake religious pilgrimages, inns also became staging posts on journeys of spiritual discovery. Perhaps most famously Geoffrey Chaucer's pilgrims, in *The Canterbury Tales*, stay at the Tabard Inn in Southwark 'Ready to go on pilgrimage and start / For Canterbury, most devout at heart'. The Tabard even gets the equivalent of an online review from the English poet: 'The rooms and stables of the inn', he writes, 'were wide: / They made us easy, all was of the best.' Similar inns were to be found the world over, their facilities altering little over the centuries but evolving and expanding in line with urbanization and maritime exploration and to meet the subsequent demands of the likes of newfangled stagecoaches and their passengers.

In the Age of Enlightenment of the eighteenth century, though, a further dimension was added when the upper classes embraced the idea of travelling for pleasure and to expand their horizons by seeing something of the world. So-called Grand Tours began to be undertaken to sites of historical, cultural, aesthetic or scenic interest by well-to-do types wishing to improve themselves and, as often as not, also let their hair down while away from the strictures of home.

The English term 'hotel', a French contraction of the word 'hostel', dates from this time – 1765 to be precise – and refers to 'an inn, especially of a superior kind.' This was, after all, the moment when a divide gradually opened up between the mostly workaday inns of old and more leisure-orientated hotels of the future. The latter at this juncture started to take a form we might recognize today, as separate dining rooms, rest rooms,

coffee lounges and the like were added for guests less pressed for time (or the rapid turnaround and timetables of a mail coach), and wishing for rather more genteel spaces to unwind and in which to dine. Assembly rooms and ballrooms for convivial socializing and events joined the mix now, too. And in the spa towns across Europe, where the aristocratic unwell and the wealthy were increasingly venturing to take cures for their health, a burgeoning number of resorts opened to cater to their needs. These sanatoriums duly helped to ensure that this medicine came with more than a spoonful of sugar into the bargain.

However, it was to be distance-shrinking revolutions in transport technology, first the railways and steamships in the nineteenth century followed by motorized vehicles and aeroplanes in the twentieth, that hotels as we know them truly came of age. The fact that some of the world's most iconic hotels, and many of the ones featured in this book, not only date from those times but are also with us still is proof of this in itself. But hotels, like the world, have come a long way since then – and perhaps never more so than in the last quarter of a century with the Internet and globalization rapidly redrawing our maps, literally and figuratively.

Our survey, therefore, is international in scope and covers a span of some 150 years, ranging from the 1870s when horse, boat, hot air balloon and rail were the only means of crossing the globe, right up to the present, when we can go anywhere virtually and our daily reality is augmented by the digital.

Yet many of the elements of their earlier history persist. As with our forebears, the modern hotel guest might be travelling for work or business, or seeking fresh inspiration or looking to improve their mental, physical and spiritual health, to relax and pamper themselves, or indulge their senses and satiate their culinary appetites. All of the hotels included here offer a chance to do all these things, and the reason for their inclusion is that in their individual and differing ways, they all do them exceptionally well.

I am sometimes asked what the difference is between a pretty good hotel and a truly great one. The defining factor is always the attitude of its employees. While many hotels offer beautiful marble finishes, exquisite decorations or prime locations, these elements alone do not elevate a hotel to greatness. The true difference lies in a commitment to service excellence, which starts with the general manager. If the general manager embodies humility, promotes the right values and maintains uncompromising service standards, the hotel will naturally ascend to greatness. How the day starts for the guest can make all the difference. Breakfast, I feel, often sets the tone. Fresh and original fare, attentive staff and a sense of everyone going the extra mile from first light leaves a lasting impression.

To become iconic, a hotel must sustain its standards of excellence, combining a premier location, state-of-the-art facilities and a consistently exceptional service culture. Service is everything. Without it, even the most luxurious hotels become ordinary – and there is nothing ordinary about any of the following hotels. They embody the best of our industry. But our survey, I hope, also tells a story about where hotels have come from and where they might be going and the changing demands of our guests. Without whom, of course, a hotel is nothing.

For older hotels, even the most august ones that have previously stood the test of time, the challenge is never about modernity but again attitude. Those who wish to survive and indeed thrive in the twenty-first century must blend historical charm with the expectations of contemporary guests. In these pages, you will find examples of classic hotels doing just that, and brilliantly. Alongside equally newer kids on the block pointing fresh directions forward.

In the coming years, AI technology will transform our lives in ways that we can barely imagine yet.

Forward-thinking hotels, old and new, are already embracing it, and using it to streamline the most basic processes from taking bookings to answering customer queries. But the human touch remains irreplaceable. I fervently believe that such technology, if used properly, should enable us to do more for our guests, allowing us to personalize our services and free us to fully focus on their individual needs and specific requests. Sustainability is another issue that concerns us all. Hotels need to be good custodians of the environment. Here you will find hotels that are genuinely making a difference to both their local ecosystem and the planet at large without being hair-shirted when it comes to fine dining and high-end creature comforts. Increasingly, guests themselves prioritize their wellbeing and look to nurture themselves while seeking hotels that offer unique local experiences. It is something that you will also see reflected here in spades.

Some of these hotels may be familiar to you, others perhaps less so, but each one is worthy of its place in these pages and well worth a visit in its own right – and I hope you leave this book wishing to do just that. Hospitality is as much a vocation as a business and hotels a way of life as well as a living for me, personally. I had the enormous pleasure of working for the legendary hotelier Horst Schulze, who was one of my great mentors during my professional career in hospitality. Schulze once outlined three steps of service. First and foremost was to offer your guests the warmest and most sincere of welcomes to make them feel valued from the outset. Secondly, a good hotelier, he felt, should always try to anticipate their guests' needs and address them proactively to ensure the whole experience appears effortless. Thirdly and finally, at the end of their stay, he advised bidding guests the fondest of farewells, guiding them to the door in person and inviting them to return. In following his advice, I welcome you to this book and trust you will have all you need here and enjoy your stay with us. Our wish, too, is that you will want to come back to us again and again.

CARSTEN K. RATH

HOTEL SACHER

VIENNA · AUSTRIA

An icon of luxury hospitality, majestically standind in the heart of Vienna, embodying elegance, tradition, and unparalleled service since 1876.

HÔTEL SACHER
HOTEL SACHER
HOTEL SACHER

Occupying some 11,473 square metres of urban land across six separate but deceptively interlinked buildings in Vienna, the Hotel Sacher is a true landmark of the Austrian capital – its place in the history and heart of this European metropolis as assured as that of the father of psychoanalysis, Sigmund Freud, or the writer Stefan Zweig. The hotel has served as the basis and setting for novels, films, a ballet and even a popular television series. But it is almost impossible not to begin with the torte. For the Hotel Sacher is synonymous the world over with its house speciality, the Original Sacher-Torte: a velvety rich chocolate cake with a dark chocolate glaze finish and a central layer of apricot jam, traditionally served as the perfect accompaniment to a coffee, with a side order of unsweetened whipped cream.

Its recipe is a closely guarded secret and one that resulted in at least two fiercely contested legal cases in the 1930s and 1950s, both of which were conclusively won by the hotel, who much later again had to see off a plagiaristic spying mission from a Japanese confectioner.

But it all goes back to 1832, when Franz Sacher, a sixteen-year-old kitchen apprentice in the household of Prince Klemens von Metternich conjured up the cake for the first time. The conservative Habsburg statesman is said to have pronounced Sacher's creation 'exquisite' – a verdict that has rung true ever since.

Franz, however, was to take his gastronomic skills elsewhere upon marrying, moving to Pressburg (now Bratislava in Slovakia), where he became the chef of the distinguished Adelige Casino restaurant before then running the catering for the Danube Steamship Company in Budapest. In the wake of the political revolutions of 1848 that would see the fall of Prince Metternich and the abdication of the authoritarian Austrian Emperor Ferdinand I, Sacher returned to Vienna, where he established a delicatessen-cum-diner that won acclaim for its fresh oysters and the quality of its wines. During this same period, and as part of his modernizing agenda, the new emperor, Franz Joseph I, was to order the razing of Vienna's old city walls, paving the way for the creation of the city's famed Ringstrasse in a radical rebuilding of the Austrian capital that equalled Georges-Eugène Haussmann's schemes for Paris. It was, nevertheless, to the French capital, and also to Lyon and London, that Sacher's second son Eduard, hungry for knowledge, was to depart to continue a culinary education that had begun in his father's deli.

While eating his way across Europe, Eduard was to take note of the emergence of such grand hotels as the Athénée and the Langham in Paris and London, respectively. Initially he set his sights on becoming a restaurateur and on arriving back in Vienna, aged just twenty-one, at first established an inn in the suburb of Döbling.

But in 1866 he obtained the lease on premises to install an innovative buffet eatery in the Palais Todesco, a new building erected on the site of one of Vienna's former gatehouses. A winning element of Eduard's establishment was its *séparées* or intimate dining rooms, a fashion he imported from Paris, where the great and the good, or the merely hungry, could exchange confidences in private while they ate and drank safely away from prying eyes (and ears) of the public. This feature was to be retained when a decade later Eduard, with the backing of four local businessmen and the government, launched himself into the hotel business. The former Kärntnertortheater – a concert venue that had previously hosted the premiere of Beethoven's 9th Symphony conducted by its composer and opposite the Court Opera House – was demolished and a hotel to a design by the architect Wilhelm Fraenkel with thirteen 'salons particuliers', or separate dining rooms, was erected in its place. This new hotel, in honour of its musical neighbour, was to be called the

◂ To walk through the doorway of the Hotel Sacher is to step into an Austrian institution of timeless elegance. Its lavish Grand Signature Suite, meanwhile, offers near 360° views of Vienna.

▸ Sumptuous but inviting, the Hotel Sacher takes comfort seriously, its lobby, like all its rooms, exuding old-world charm updated for contemporary sensibilities.

ORIGINAL
SACHER
TORTE

ORIGINAL
SACHER
TORTE

Hôtel de l'Opéra for its first two decades, though its restaurant bore the Sacher name on its opening in 1876; both were to prove an immediate hit with high society.

Four years later, Eduard, already a thirty-seven-year-old widower, was to marry Anna Maria Fuchs, sixteen years his junior and the daughter of a prosperous Leopoldstadt butcher. From the outset, Anna was involved in the business and in the aftermath of Eduard's comparatively early death in 1892, she was to become the hotel's dynamic and exacting driving force. Once quizzed about her status by a guest wishing to speak to the manager, a post they had assumed must be held by a man, she responded, 'I am *the* Sacher!' To the whole of Belle Époque Vienna, and to her regular patrons, indeed she was. She cut quite a figure, too, with a mop of curly hair, constantly puffing on Havana cigars and forever trailed at the ankles by one of her beloved French bulldogs.

The author Felix Salten, a frequent diner at the hotel's restaurant Rote Bar and whose 1923 book, *Bambi*, was later adapted into the much-loved Walt Disney animation, remembered Anna as 'such a darling ... brilliant, seemingly grumpy but with an impish face alive with a thousand mischievous thoughts'. It was Anna who initiated one of the Sacher's enduring traditions: embroidering the signatures of distinguished visitors onto the hotel's damask tablecloths. This began after a dinner for Archduke Otto, brother to the unfortunate Archduke Franz Ferdinand who would be assassinated in Sarajevo in 1914. Having enjoyed a sumptuous repast in his favourite *séparée*, Otto appeared in a particularly relaxed mood. Seizing her moment, Anna approached him with a fresh tablecloth and got him to sign it. She personally embroidered the result on the cloth to preserve it. This regal precedent set, she went on to gather over four hundred signatures from the cream of Austro-Hungarian society and beyond. The cloth would end up bearing witness to the turn of global events. One once treasured signatory, the Grand Duke Nicholas Nikolaevich, went on to lead the Imperial Russian Army against Austria and Germany in the First World War.

The Sacher has been on safer ground in more recent decades. The likes of the great calypso singer and civil rights activist Harry Belafonte, the actor Sir Anthony Hopkins, and American presidential candidate and former first lady Hillary Clinton are among the notable additions to the Sacher's signature cloth collection in modern times. This sewing tradition is upheld in honour of the remarkable Anna, a woman who valued history and time-honoured crafts but had an eye on posterity yet was always looking to the future. She was to die in her room in the hotel in 1930, aged seventy-one after forty odd years at the helm. Over ten thousand people came to pay their last respects to her and mourn the loss of one of Vienna's most characterful and successful hoteliers.

In the year after Anna's death, the silent screen legend Charlie Chaplin chose the Sacher's bar as a discrete bolthole to catch up with old friends, including the composer Oscar Straus. It was one of the few places in Vienna he could slip into safely and avoid the over-eager attentions of the thousands of fans who had earlier gathered to greet his incoming train

◀ No visit to the Hotel Sacher is complete without sampling its world famous Original Sacher-Torte. A symbol of Austrian confectionery since its creation in 1832, it is typically served with a dollop of unsweetened cream and perfectly accompanies a demitasse of strong Viennese coffee.

▲ The inimitable Anna Sacher, here with her beloved French bulldogs, assumed the management of the hotel on the death of her husband, Eduard, in 1892. Her style, energy and attention to detail helped make the Sacher what it is today.

HOTEL SACHER
HOTEL SACHER
RESTAURANT
EDUARD SACHER
HOTEL SACHER
SACHER

◂ Centrally situated and offering breathtaking views of such historic landmarks as St Stephen's Cathedral and the renowned Vienna State Opera, the Hotel Sacher puts the city in instant reach.

▴ Another tradition that dates back to Anna Sacher is the collecting of photographs and memorabilia of famous guests. Pictures and keepsakes from distinguished visitors, past and present, remain a charming feature of the hotel's elegant interior decor, making first timers feel part of this rich lineage.

from Berlin. The playwright, songwriter and wit Noël Coward was another British movie star who came to the hotel in this period. While the then British monarch, Edward VIII, lunched at the Sacher during an official state visit in 1936, just months before his abdication and scandalous marriage to the American divorcee Mrs Wallis Simpson. He was subsequently to return to the Sacher as a guest, checking in with his wife under their new titles, the Duke and Duchess of Windsor. His niece, Queen Elizabeth II, would eventually pay her own visit to the Sacher, attending a dinner after a night at the opera some thirty years later.

But the 1930s were to be a bleak decade, economically and politically. The Sacher itself teetered on the brink of bankruptcy in the aftermath of the Wall Street Crash. It was only saved thanks to the intervention of a pair of married couples; the lawyer Dr Hans Gürtler and his wife, Poldi, and the café owner Joseph Siller and his wife, Anna, none of whom could bear to see it close. They were to launch renovation work that saw the installation of hot and cold running water, central heating and electricity to all the rooms that gave the hotel a new lease of life. Sadly darker clouds were on the horizon, and Austria was annexed by Nazi Germany on 13 March 1938.

The Hotel Sacher fortunately came through the Second World War relatively unscathed and avoided the fate of the nearby State Opera House, which was destroyed by an incendiary bomb and had to be completely rebuilt. Though, on the city's liberation, the Rote Bar briefly served as a stable for horses of the Red Army. Once the blitz dust had settled, post-war Vienna was divided into four different occupation zones, each under the control of the Allied forces of either France, the United States, the United Kingdom or the Soviet Union. The Sacher, located in the British sector, was consequently commandeered for the Senior Officers' Transit Club. Accordingly the restored Rote Bar restaurant was to witness gatherings of the Beefsteak Club, where each month a group of British dinners met to feast on oxtail soup, plum pudding and similar fare, each meal concluding with port and a toast to the king.

The novelist Graham Greene was to write the screenplay of *The Third Man* while staying at the Sacher in 1948. This classic film noir directed by Carol Reed and shot on location the following year in Vienna's bomb-pockmarked streets (and its sewers) starred Orson Welles as the black-market racketeer Harry Lime. Welles was also a guest of the hotel during the shoot, commending the Sacher's head barman, Ernst Badorf, for making 'the best Bloody Mary in the world'.

It was not until 1951, however, that something approaching normal service was resumed and the hotel was handed back to its rightful owners, members of the Gürtler and Siller families, whose descendants remain its custodians to this day.

In some respects, it might be easier to list those who have not stayed at the Sacher in the intervening decades since the roll call ranges from the actors Gary Cooper, Jack Lemmon, Alain Delon and Romy

From the Café Sacher to each of its 152 rooms and suites, the Hotel Sacher wears the refinement of its fin-de-siècle origins with ease but embraces the modern with state-of-the-art facilities and fittings.

Schneider, Elizabeth Taylor and Liza Minnelli, to the conductor Sir Georg Solti, rock 'n' roller Bill Haley and Beatle John Lennon and his wife, the artist Yoko Ono, who staged one of their bed-ins in their suite.

When asked to select a famous guest that best sums up the spirit of the Sacher, they suggest Grace Kelly – the screen goddess who rose from humble origins to become first a Hollywood star and then Princess of Monaco, a role of service that she performed with equal attention to excellence without forgetting her modest roots. The Sacher's own story, after all, as they point out, began with a mere kitchen apprentice. Soon enough, the hotel was playing host to King Milan of Serbia and countless other crowned heads of Europe, while the Austro-Hungarian Empress Sisi had the Original Sacher-Torte delivered, near daily, to her palace.

It is a testament to the contemporary management that some of the concierge staff have over twenty years' experience of working at the hotel. And whilst being custodians of its dear heritage, everyone has adapted to the changing tastes and range of guests, their current duties aided by the latest digital tools. The Sacher has old world elegance in spades. Its present visitors, nevertheless, naturally expect and receive all the modern amenities of high-speed internet access, in-room entertainment systems and luxurious bathrooms amid the immaculately preserved period features. The Original Sacher-Torte reigns supreme – 365,000 cakes are produced every year and they are now shipped the world over. But spa facilities offering cutting-edge wellness services and health-conscious options on the hotel menu cater for those seeking to nourish themselves less decadently. Traditionalists, however, have nothing to fear. The familiar comforts of flaky-pastry home-made apple strudel and golden Wiener schnitzel, served with a tangy cranberry sauce and potatoes, are still on the bill of fare, flying the flag for Viennese culinary culture just as they did in Anna Sacher's day. The establishment's rather more relaxed dress codes might well shock her, but this shrewd businesswoman would surely be delighted by many of the newer innovations. She would most likely be pleased, too, to see that the standards she set are more than maintained – those tablecloth signatures continuing to be hand-stitched – and that the hotel and the torte she knew from the refined era of grad waltzes by Strauss still thrive in our AI-enabled present.

The legendary Hollywood actor and director Orson Welles proclaimed the Bloody Marys at the Sacher 'the best in the world'. Whatever your tipple, you can sample it while drinking in the unique ambience of each of its restaurant bars: the Grüne Bar, canopied by a Lobmeyr chandelier – hallmark of traditional Viennese craftsmanship – offers regional dishes; enjoy cocktails and apéritifs amidst the brocade walls of the Blau Bar, and delicious coffee and confectionary in the opulent two-floored Café Bel Étage.

VIER JAHRES-ZEITEN

HAMBURG · GERMANY

The epitome of European luxury hotels, this elegant place on the Inner Alster Lake has provided guests from all corners of globe with a world-class welcome all year round since 1897.

At this point in time, we take it as read that any hotel, from the most luxurious to the lowliest, will offer hot water and central heating. But this was far from the case only a century or so ago. In 1900, Hotel Vier Jahreszeiten became the first establishment in Hamburg to be able to offer them as standard to guests when a then cutting-edge water-heating system was installed by its forward-thinking founding owner Friedrich Haerlin. As reflected in its name, a reference to the 'four seasons', the hotel was intended to be open all-year round. The winters in Hamburg, one of the world's great port cities in the north of Germany, on the banks of the River Elbe, are relatively mild when compared to, say, Berlin. Even so, hot water and central heating make the coastal winters a good deal more appealing, and they helped Haerlin, who personally suffered from bronchial complaints in cold and damp conditions, to fulfil his promise of providing unsurpassed levels of comfort for his guests from January to December, no matter how unseasonal the weather.

Born in the Stuttgart suburb of Gaisburg in 1857, Friedrich was the youngest son of a local baker and innkeeper left bankrupt in the so-called 'Founders' Crisis' stock market crash of 1873. With the family finances wiped out, Haerlin, armed with a small suitcase and fifty marks in his pocket, headed to Switzerland to improve his prospects. He wound up working as an office boy in the restaurant at Geneva railway station but gained a firmer grounding in hospitality as a waiter in Chantepoulet, a smart café-restaurant in Baden, before eventually – via various positions in hotels as far afield as London and the south of France – becoming the manager of the Bellevue in Bern. It was at the Bellevue that he also met his wife and business partner, Thekla Toussaint. A feisty twenty-four-year-old amateur sportswoman from a Bremen hat-factory-owning family, Toussaint was staying at the hotel over the New Year celebrations of 1891. After a romance largely conducted at a distance and by correspondence, the couple married just over two years later and began running another hotel together in Thun.

For the second time, though, a bankruptcy changed the course of Friedrich's life. On this occasion, however, fate smiled upon him. On the eve of his fortieth birthday in February 1897, he learnt that Hotel Vier Jahreszeiten in Hamburg had gone bust and was being sold the next day at auction. Encouraged by Thekla, Friedrich decided to put in a bid. One waved finger later and the birthday boy emerged from the auction rooms some 420,000 marks lighter but the proud owner of a modest hotel of just eleven rooms and three bathrooms on the Neu Jungfernstieg overlooking the Inner Alster Lake. By 1909, with the stealthy purchase of neighbouring properties and astute cultivation of an appreciative clientele, Hotel Vier Jahreszeiten had swelled to over 140 rooms and could luxuriate under the title of a 'grand' hotel and would become grander still in the decades, some politically turbulent, to come when further neighbouring premises were acquired.

But in 1913, the sixteen-year-old Fritz, the youngest of Friedrich and Thekla's three sons, joined the staff of the hotel. Fritz was the only one of the couple's sons to return from the First World War and went on to succeed his father as manager in 1932. He was later aided in this endeavour by his own wife, Agnes, and their two daughters, Annemarie and Thekla, and the hotel stayed in the family's hands right up until 1989 – the year the Berlin Wall fell. It has had only two further owners since, and the hotel's motto remains, as it was in Friedrich's day, 'Service, Service, Service'. Ingo C. Peters, Hotel Vier Jahreszeiten's present director, got his first break at the hotel as a kitchen hand in 1981 and returned from studying and working in America to take up the reins as manager some sixteen years later; he has been in at the helm for nearly three decades now.

◀ Beginning with just a small building of eleven rooms on Hamburg's Neuer Jungfernstieg, Hotel Vier Jahreszeiten soon blossomed to become what it remains today, a much-loved establishment of 156 rooms and suites that is widely regarded as one of classiest hotels in Europe.

▶ The lobby at Hotel Vier Jahreszeiten, its reception staff trim in the black jackets that have been the standard uniform here for generations and another of the charming traditions it maintains while also moving with the times.

NT HAERLIN
ROYAL SERVICE
RECEPTION

The main entrance to Hotel Vier Jahreszeiten on Neuer Jungfernstieg in 1930, shortly before its founder Friedrich Haerlin handed the hotel over to his son, Fritz, to run.

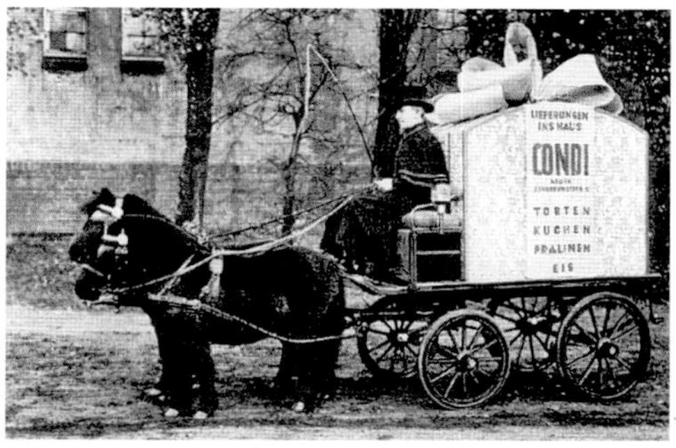

Top: Seagulls circle above neatly turned-out hotel staff on a balcony facing out onto the Inner Alster Lake.

Bottom right to left: A liveried horse-drawn coach carrying deliveries from Café Condi, the hotel's cake shop and coffee house, and an exterior shot of the hotel from 1930; and the interior of its main hall in 1913.

HOTEL
VIER JAHRESZEITEN
HAMBURG

Under both Friedrich's and Fritz's tenures, the hotel sourced nearly all of its produce – meat, eggs and vegetables, along with flowers for buttonholes and table decorations – from a farm and kitchen garden that the Haerlins owned on the outskirts of the city. While today's hotel no longer has its own dedicated farm, it endeavours, in the interest of sustainability, to obtain as much of its food and products as possible from Hamburg and the surrounding areas. The hotel still promotes the Schlemmerschnitte, a classic North German speciality of steak tartare on buttered brown toast served with a side salad, and caviar as an optional extra, as its trademark dish.

Its main eatery, the Michelin-starred Restaurant Haerlin, still bears the name it was given to honour Friedrich back in 1919. The Condi, a Biedermeier-style coffee house and cake shop established by Fritz in 1934 meanwhile keeps the best breakfasts in town coming, as it has done for ninety odd years.

Yet Hotel Vier Jahreszeiten can hardly be said to have stood still. It has always adapted to the changing expectations of its guests, as is evidenced by its adoption of everything from central heating in the last century to pan-Asian menu options more recently. Rightly predicting a greater interest in health treatments in the twenty-first century, it launched its fifth and sixth floor Vier Jahreszeiten Spa & Fitness centre at the turn of millennium. A few years later, with the trend for al fresco dining on the march, it opened the Jahreszeiten Terrasse on the Inner Alster for refreshments in spring air and summer sun with spectacular panoramic boulevard views of the Jungfernstieg and the Ballindamm. In 2015, all of its 156 rooms and suites, restaurants and wellness areas were extensively modernized in its biggest refit to date, and in 2021, the hotel's capacious and well-stocked wine cellar (itself a legacy from the investments Fritz made in decent Bordeaux in 1933), was reborn as an exclusive and stylish event venue.

Guests these days can also opt to stay in one of the hotel's 'celebrity' suites, each named and themed after such illustrious visitors of the past as the actor Peter Ustinov, the fashion designer Ralph Lauren and the opera diva Maria Callas. That the notoriously demanding Callas chose to stay here again and again arguably tells you all you need to know about Hotel Vier Jahreszeiten and its commitment to customer satisfaction.

◂ The relaxation area of the Vier Jahreszeiten Spa & Fitness centre and the hotel's open-air roof terrace provide conducive spaces for guests to unwind.

▴ Pleasure cruisers passing the hotel on the Inner Alster in 1930.

The fourth floor Presidential Suite offers a breathtaking panoramic view over the Inner Alster and maximum comfort over a truly expansive two-hundred-square-metre domain.

◂ Newer additions to the hotel's culinary venues include the wine cellar and the recently revamped Grill restaurant.

▸ The Michelin-starred Restaurant Haerlin opened in 1919 and it is still going strong.

RESTAURANT HAERLIN

The Alster Suite is lakeside luxury personified, a room with a view that is first rate whatever the season.

THE DOLDER GRAND

ZURICH · SWITZERLAND

Magnificent views over Zurich,
the lake and the Alps and
an art collection boasting more than
one hundred works, including originals
by Niki de Saint Phalle and Salvador Dalí,
it has to be seen to be believed.

With a lofty location in the Adlisberg mountains, the Dolder Grand has been a treasured feature of the Zurich landscape ever since it first opened in 1899. Its original building was restored to its former glory in a radical renovation undertaken between 2004 and 2008 by the acclaimed London-based architects Foster + Partners, which also saw two brand new wings added that brought a contemporary dimension to the historical building.

ZURICH · SWITZERLAND

It was the Romantics in the late eighteenth and early nineteenth centuries who found beauty in the alpine landscape of Switzerland, glorying in the wildness of a sublime mountain scenery that previously had largely been judged chaotic and terrifying. In their wake, sightseers and sportsmen seeking to commune with divine nature, scale the great peaks or ski down the icy slopes followed. Their passages to formerly remote areas were eventually eased by the arrival of the railways in the 1840s. Around the same time, doctors began hymning the benefits of fresh alpine air to those afflicted by then common respiratory diseases like tuberculosis, in turn attracting visitors looking to improve their health in general. It was both of these groups that Heinrich Hürlimann, the Swiss restaurateur and entrepreneur, had consciously in mind when he began drawing up his plans to build a new hotel and *Curhaus* (literally 'cure house' or health retreat) some two kilometres outside Zurich and on a woody foothill of the Adlisberg around two hundred metres above the city. The setting alone was breathtaking, with spectacular views of the metropolis and of the pellucid waters of Lake Zurich below. But it was also practical, as the hotel would be served by a recently opened station at Dolderbahn and a rack-and-pinion railway. Hürlimann would, he believed, have the best of both worlds here: his guests would be uniquely close to nature with the forest and mountain on their doorstep and yet near enough to the city to feel that urban life had not been abandoned entirely.

For the hotel itself Hürlimann turned to the architect Jacques Gros. Gros was the son of a landscape gardener who had studied and completed his architectural apprenticeship in Basel before eventually founding his own firm in Zurich. Akin to the Arts and Crafts movement in Britain, Gros was part of a generation of Swiss architects who looked to the vernacular historic style of the nation's rustic wooden farmhouses and chalets for inspiration. His design for Dolder Grand Hotel & Curhaus combined his veneration for and knowledge of alpine timber construction with modernist Art Nouveau elements to produce an almost fairy-castle-like structure comprised of a central tower with a needle spire and two large asymmetric wings garnished with regal turrets. That the animator Walt Disney, whose own home in Los Feliz, California, was built in the fantastical Storybook style of architecture, is among a litany of its subsequent famous guests, which also include Winston Churchill, Sophia Loren and Nelson Mandela, seems only appropriate really.

Opening in May 1899, Dolder Grand Hotel & Curhaus initially boasted some 220 beds, a reading and billiards room, a café-restaurant, covered verandas and terraces, and what were then still modern marvels such as lifts (two, no less) and telephones. Eight years later, a section of nearby parkland on the southern slope of the Adlisberg was transformed into a picturesque nine-hole golf course. This was one of the first courses in Switzerland, but the sport had been growing in popularity as a pursuit for the leisured and well-heeled in Britain and also in America, where it was embraced by the Gilded Age elite, with soon to be world famous clubs like Brookline, Wheaton, Shinnecock Hills and Saint Andrew's, Hastings-on-Hudson, all founded in the late 1800s. The Dolder course, though short, is respected by golfers, professional and amateur alike, all around the world, as a pleasingly demanding one. Its steeped greens, slopes and bunkers, which were updated in 2005, and the surrounding thickets of forest trees, make a game on it physically and mentally challenging, but immensely satisfying too.

A perfect combination architecturally of the classic and the modern, the Dolder Grand's buildings and interiors range from the traditional to the cutting edge, each with ambiences as inviting as they are unique.

The Dolder Grand is much more than just a place for guests to stay the night. The hotel on the Adlisberg is a social hub, a melting pot, and one of Switzerland's top addresses when it comes to culinary delights. Its lobby and the Bar regularly host the local and international scene, who flock to the Dolder Grand to network, socialise and enjoy a drink with friends in a laid-back atmosphere. The Dolder Grand treats its guests to a unique ambience in its 175 rooms and suites, all of which boast elaborate designs full of sophisticated details. Each of them exudes its own, individual combination of elegance and exclusivity. All the deluxe double rooms in the historic main building and new extension wings are south-facing, their refined and spacious interiors consistently illuminated by natural light. All rooms and suites share a wonderful sense of space. To round off an unforgettable living experience, guests of the Dolder Grand get to take in sweeping views.

Switzerland may have stayed neutral in the First World War, but in its aftermath and following the global influenza pandemic of 1918/19, even more emphasis began to be placed on the benefits of sunlight, fresh air and outdoor exercise for health: skating, swimming and sunbathing came into vogue in the 1920s and 1930s as never before. These new leisure activities were met in 1931 by a newly commissioned Kunsteisbahn, an open-air ice-skating rink to a state-of-the-art design by the architects Witzig and Begert, that was built in walking distance from the hotel. It was to be the largest and most technically advanced rink in Europe and went on to host the World Figure Skating Championships each February for many years. Occupying an area of six thousand square metres, a current rink run in conjunction with the city of Zurich is its worthy successor and every winter provides the same thrill of skating in this stunning alpine location.

Three years after the creation of the Kunsteisbahn, the Dolder Grand opened a wave pool nearby in the midst of a clearing of beach and fir trees. This offered visitors the chance of 'bathing in crystal-clear basin water, kept at a constant temperature' with gently lapping 'artificial waves' and a place for 'hygienic' exercise 'in ozone-rich mountain air'. The pool was the work of the architect Emil Rein and a modernist masterpiece of crisp, clean streamlined styling that was to serve as the backdrop not only for sporting contests like national swimming championships but also for fashion shows and dance events. Such summer revels came to a halt with the outbreak of the Second World War when trade to the hotel dried up almost entirely. The Dolder Grand endured a lean decade before flourishing once more in the1950s and 1960s when a new building by Hans von Meyenburg was added to cope with the demand, and the hotel has never looked back since.

Whereas in the post-war period, the hotel answered guests' demands for ensuite bathrooms and car parking spaces and diversified into providing conferencing services for the international great and the good, in the past decade, the Dolder Grand has adopted robots to speed up delivering of some basic housekeeping services, freeing its staff to provide more hands-on care of visitors, and it was the first hotel in Switzerland to accept payment in cryptocurrency.

An inventive but sensitive expansion in the early 2000s, however, under the aegis of star British architect Norman Foster, successfully put Gros's founding building back at the heart of the complex. It also further emphasized the continuum between hotel and *Curhaus* of old and the present day with the addition of a new spa and medical wellness centre, whose facilities, at the time of writing, are spread over some four thousand square metres, making it the largest in Zurich. A century on, Hürlimann's basic formula for the Dolder Grand appears in robust health, especially as ever more people seek destinations that offer scope to improve themselves, in one way or another, as well as unwind. The Dolder Grand provides bags of options for both.

In addition to mountain views, sport and fresh air, the hotel has over the years accumulated a fine private collection of art for guests to immerse themselves in, with over a hundred works, including paintings, sculptures and installations, from the likes of Salvador Dalí, Henry Moore and Niki de Saint Phalle. With five restaurants to choose from, including a garden restaurant for vegetarians and vegan gourmands and refined Asian dishes in an Omakase restaurant, the hotel's Michelin-starred menus reflect its head chef Heiko Nieder's commitment to combining traditional techniques with modern influences to produce upscale cuisine that is outward-looking but seasonal, regional and responsible. These final four words could apply equally to the Dolder Grand itself, a hotel that is a Zurich landmark and quintessentially Swiss but which welcomes the world with a form of luxury hospitality that is holistic and life-enhancing.

Fine dining has always been the order of the day at the Dolder Grand, here guests at a banquet in the 1950s tuck into a sumptuous buffet. Today visitors have five restaurants to choose between and Michelin-starred menus to suit every palate with gourmet vegan and Asian dishes among the options.

The Dolder Grand's main building with its iconic central spire and twin turrets under construction in the 1890s.

Sketched plans done on a paper napkin for its arresting new additions by Norman Foster from around 2004.

Historic photographs of the Dolder Grand's dedicated streetcar in 1905 and its main dining room and fully equipped kitchens in the 1970s, the latter an era when the likes of the Shah of Iran and the American diplomat Henry Kissinger and the Hollywood stars Roger Moore, John Wayne and Sophia Loren all stayed at the hotel.

This astonishing stained-glass tableau in the Steinhalle and entitled *The Chapel of Remorse* is by the contemporary Finnish artist Jani Leinonen and is just one of the over a hundred works of art in the hotel's private collection. On the pages that follow: the lobby, which doubles as an art gallery, and throughout the hotel interior, spaces feature pieces by the likes of Salvador Dalí, Fernando Botero, Joan Miró, Max Ernst, Keith Haring and Sylvester Stallone, among many others.

21 November 1996
← ENVY

The Steinhalle's chandelier, staircase, statuary and landscape paintings highlight the hotel's more classical side, while its main building balconies and the floor-to-ceiling windows of some of its newer suites help to put real-life nature in the picture.

THE TAJ MAHAL PALACE

MUMBAI · INDIA

An integral part of Mumbai's history and part of its heart and soul, this grand hotel is a local landmark and truly Indian institution.

◂ The Taj Mahal's Indo-Saracenic Revival style frontage illuminated at night and as viewed from the poolside

▾ The hotel's majestic central red dome backdropped by the Arabian Sea.

▸ The interior of the central dome with its decor recalling centuries of Indian artistry.

At a time when the world was still carved up between colonial powers, one man dreamed of creating a place of lasting beauty, where all would feel welcome, regardless of colour or creed. That place is the Taj Mahal Palace Hotel. When founded, India was still under British rule and most of the big hotels across the subcontinent operated a colour bar that excluded non-European guests. Yet more than build a hotel, Jamsetji Tata, the visionary Indian entrepreneur who founded Tata – the globally renowned conglomerate and today worth billions – with a single textile mill in central India, wanted to create something that would attract people to India and enhance life in Mumbai. What he built would surpass the grandest of all grand hotels.

Tata was to lavish nearly £300,000 on this pet project, an utterly staggering sum for the period, while members of his family and business associates all counselled against wasting his money on such an obvious white elephant.

But when it opened its doors on 16 December 1903, the hotel, built in the ornate Indo-Saracenic Revival style of architecture, was a revelation. If recalling Rajput palaces of old with its red domed roof, it was the first fully electrified building in Mumbai and the first with a lift, ice-making machine and mechanized laundry. It was also – and remains over 120 years later – an establishment of bravura magnificence and the pride of Apollo Bunder – the harbour-side area formerly occupied by docks and wharves, where the British would also erect their Gateway of India, a stately monumental welcoming arch conceived for King George V and his queen, Alexandra, on their official visit to the country in 1911 to commemorate his recent coronation as Emperor of India.

Jamsetji Tata is memorialized with a suite bearing his name, the Tata Suite, perhaps the most bountiful room that the hotel offers, its interiors highlighting the richness of India's historic craft and ornamentation with Makrana white marble floors, intricate timber marquetry and gloriously patterned Indian hand-knotted carpets.

Another luminary similarly honoured is the revered Indian musician Ravi Shankar. In 1966, his pupil George Harrison of the Beatles checked into the Taj Mahal Palace under an assumed name and began taking lessons here from the doyen of the sitar and his protégé Shambhu Das. Harrison relishing the opportunity to learn from these masters in the quiet seclusion the hotel, safely away from the attentions of screaming fans. The Ravi Shankar Suite therefore celebrates this meeting of Eastern and Western musical minds. It comes with rare memorabilia from the Shankar foundation archive and a library of recordings by both artists. Its interior decor, which includes photographs of the Beatles in India, explicitly pays tribute to the colours of toona wood, a type of reddish mahogany, from which most sitars are made.

Even before this encounter, however, the hotel already had quite an event-filled history. During the First World War, it was converted into a hospital. Mahatma Gandhi, who successfully led the peaceful campaign against British colonial rule, gave a speech in its ballroom demanding independence. And Lord Louis Mountbatten, the last British viceroy of India, made his departing address here, too, in 1947.

In the 1970s, a new high-rise wing was added to the hotel. If not to everyone's taste, the far more modern rooms in the Tower side of the hotel are fitted with floor-to-ceiling plate glass windows that provide some of the finest views of Mumbai and the Arabian Sea. The duality of the hotel, one side regal and enjoyably old-fashioned, the other gleaming and up to date, mirror the city it serves, which is India's cultural and financial powerhouse, as it is home to both the National Stock Exchange and its film industry.

The striking main staircase and hallways, light, airy and graceful, are spaces to linger rather than hurry through.

More recently and tragically, the hotel was a target in the Mumbai terrorist attacks of 2008. Thirty-one people died within the hotel, among them guests and staff, many of who perished while valiantly trying to escort visitors to safety. The hotel's dog, Lucy, also fell victim. That the hotel was chosen only underscores its central place in the heart of Mumbai. The Taj Mahal Palace, like Mumbai itself, rebounded from the outrage stronger than ever and continues to be the destination of choice for well-heeled overseas visitors and upscale local families alike. Aside from its extravagantly and eclectically themed suites and rooms, which scale from the aforementioned 'Presidential' to 'Signature' and 'Grand Luxury' down to the merely 'Luxury Executive', the hotel houses arguably the best swimming pool in the city and both its afternoon tea and the impeccable service of its staff are legendary. There is a substantial spa that specializes in Ayurvedic treatments.

The recently introduced restaurant Loya celebrates India's rich culinary heritage by retracing the timeless techniques, heirloom ingredients and evocative flavours from the grand terrains of the northern Subcontinent. The cuisines of Japan, the Eastern Mediterranean and China are also available, respectively, from Wasabi by Morimoto, the Tower's rooftop Souk and the Golden Dragon. Coffee and cakes are the order of the day in La Patisserie. For something stronger, the hotel's Harbour Bar is said to be the oldest licensed bar in Mumbai and presents the chance to sample its eponymous signature cocktail – a blend of gin and local fruit juices topped off with flaming cognac – as boats and yachts sail by outside. If that is not enough, the designer boutiques and bijoux eateries of the fashionable Kala Ghoda are just a short walk away. Though frankly, the Taj Mahal Palace – which also contains an English-language bookshop, its own branch of Starbucks and a shopping arcade with outlets by Louis Vuitton, Montblanc and Christian Dior – is abundant enough on its own. Once through its doors, you could easily be forgiven for never wishing to leave its spicily scented and stunningly pampering interiors ever again.

◀ The cooling waters of the outdoor pool in front of the hotel façade.

▲ The Taj Mahal photographed in the interwar years, when it remained a byword for twentieth-century modernity in Mumbai.

Lined with photographs of the celebrities who have visited the Taj Mahal since it first opened, the Shamiana café-restaurant offers an all-day dining experience with an international à la carte menu to suit every mood and palate.

RECEPTION OFFICE

Queen Elizabeth II outside the Taj Mahal Hotel on her first state visit to India in 1961.

Top: The legendary champion world heavyweight boxer Muhammad Ali admiring the view from the balcony of his suite at the Taj Mahal Hotel in 1980. Bottom left: Jamsetji Tata, the visionary Indian entrepreneur who founded the Taj Mahal Hotel; bottom middle: an advert from 1938 for the cabaret artiste Madame Pompadour's groundbreaking, glamorous designer fashion show night at the hotel; bottom right: American astronaut Neil Armstrong and his colleagues on a stay at the Taj Mahal Hotel in October 1969 with their visit to India part of a global tour in the wake of their historic moon landing mission earlier that year.

MENU

Hors d'Oeuvre Taj

—

Creme Amandine
Consomme Madrilene en Gelee

—

Supreme de Pomfret Alice

TAJ MAHAL HOTEL

XMAS EVE
(Thursday, 24th December, 1931)
CLASSICAL CONCERT
(11-30 a.m. to 1-30 p.m.)
HANS HIMMER'S VIENNESE ORCHESTRA.
GALA NIGHT
"FETE ESPAGNOLE"
CABARET ARTISTES
POMPADOUR
(Personality Girl)
and
POMPADOUR FOLLIES
NINA & JACQUES
(The famous Continental Cabaret Dancers)
IN
Attractive Cabaret Items.
(Extension till 2 a.m.).
GALA FAVOURS
Dinner Rs. 15.
HANS HIMMER'S VIENNESE DANCE BAND.

CHRISTMAS DAY
(Friday, 25th December, 1931)
CLASSICAL CONCERT
(11-30 a.m. to 1-30 p.m.)
HANS HIMMER'S VIENNESE ORCHESTRA.
DINNE . DAI CE AND CABARET
Artistes
NINA & JACQUES
(The famous Continental Cabaret Dancers)
in
Attractive Cabaret Items.
(Extension till 1 a.m.)
Dinner Rs. 8.
HANS HIMMER'S VIENNESE DANCE BAND.

BOXING DAY
Saturday, 26th December

NEW YEAR'S EVE
(Thursday, 31st December, 1931).
CLASSICAL CONCERT
(11-30 a.m. to 1-30 p.m.).
HANS HIMMER'S VIENNESE ORCHESTRA.
GALA NIGHT
"FETE APACHE"
CABARET ARTISTES
POMPADOUR
(Personality Girl)
&
POMPADOUR FOLLIES
NINA & JACQUES
(The famous Continental Cabaret Dancers)
IN
Attractive Cabaret Items
(Extension till 2 a.m.).
CARNIVAL NOVELTIES.
Dinner Rs. 15.
HANS HIMMER'S VIENNESE DANCE BAND.

NEW YEAR
(Friday, 1st January, 1932)
CLASSICAL CONCERT
(11-30 a.m. to 1-30 p.m.).
HANS HIMMER'S VIENNESE ORCHESTRA.

Top left: The Taj Mahal's very first menu from 1903. Top right: A chef working his magic in the Zodiac Grill. Opened in 1989, this famed eatery pioneered the concept of fine European dining in Mumbai. Bottom left: A menu from 1919; middle, The hotel's seasonal fayre for the 1933 holiday season; and bottom right: This 1940s programme finds the Taj Mahal in thrall to the tango and flamenco with a Grand Gala Dance, an event infused with the spirit of a 'Latin American Fiesta'.

▶ The Golden Dragon, India's first Sichuan and Cantonese restaurant, offers cuisine to delight diners seeking dishes from across China.

The Taj Mahal Palace's corridor lined with lush plants and comfy lounge chairs.

▶ The Taj Mahal Palace's galleried upper floors.

MANDARIN ORIENTAL HYDE PARK, LONDON

LONDON · GREAT BRITAIN

Of the urban and the pastoral, Mandarin Oriental Hyde Park, London, sits on the stately city thoroughfare of Knightsbridge, amid the royal verdure of Hyde Park.

MANDARIN ORIENTAL HYDE PARK, LONDON

BALLROOM
BALLROOM
LOADING ONLY

First advertised as occupying 'The Finest Position in London', Mandarin Oriental Hyde Park, London, certainly has one of the city's smartest addresses. Located at Number 66 on the regal thoroughfare of Knightsbridge, opposite the Harvey Nichols department store, a minute's walk from Harrods and with the Victoria and Albert Museum and the Natural History Museum on its doorstep, the hotel is also in leafy old Hyde Park. Indeed, its rear terrace garden is technically part of this historic royal parkland, an expanse of verdure where King Henry VIII once hunted deer. If open to the general public since the seventeenth century, Hyde Park is still owned by the Crown, and it was a subsequent monarch, King George V, and his ban on advertising signage facing the park, that resulted in the Hyde Park Hotel switching its original front entrance from the parkside Albert Gate to Knightsbridge. But then the hotel had first been built in 1889 as the Hyde Park Court, an exclusive block of flats for upper-class bachelors; 'men', as its promoter, the speculative builder, financier, Liberal politician and later convicted fraudster Jabez Balfour put it, 'of first-class social standing, but whose means may not permit them to go to a great expense in housekeeping'.

Its architects were the then well-regarded London firm of Thomas Archer and Arthur Green, who had already designed another apartment building for single gentlemen on much the same lavish lines as for Balfour: Whitehall Court on the Embankment near the reconstructed Houses of Parliament. At a hundred feet in height, Hyde Park Court, however, was to be the tallest building in London at the time and with its baronial turrets, balconies and pillared porticos, one intended to impress – and it still does. But within nine years of its completion, and amid the collapse of Balfour's crooked business empire, the property fell into administration. It was then sold to Herbert Bennett, a director of Harrods, who, after a fire in the building, set about converting it into a hotel which opened as the Hyde Park Hotel in 1902. Where a discreet brass plaque might have done to mark the entrance of a gentlemen's apartment block, a hotel needs to be rather more noticeable. And it was here that plans for a large gilt lettered sign spelling out the hotel's name on its frontage fell foul of the king's ruling, so the whole axis of the building was switched. Its old parkside entrance was retained but reserved for the exclusive use of the royal family – which remains the case to this day, with special permission still required to allow VIPs and special wedding parties the rare chance to step through doors normally fit only for kings and queens.

The hotel's associations with the British aristocracy run deep. During the First World War, when soldiers were billeted on camp beds in its ballroom, Queen Mary was a frequent visitor. In its aftermath, both the late Queen Elizabeth II and her sister The Princess Margaret were given dance lessons in the same room, which is fitted with a sprung floor, by a Madame Vacani, who apparently instructed the little princesses to 'hold their darling little heads up'. How much the times had changed – in Henry VIII's times, such a remark to the heir to the throne could well have resulted in a loss of the instructor's own head. In addition to native notables – who included the wartime prime minister, Winston Churchill – The King of Sweden, the silent film star Rudolph Valentino and Mahatma Gandhi, the campaigner for Indian independence whose strict diet required a goat to be milked daily for him, were among the international celebrities who stayed here in first half of the twentieth century.

Shortly before the outbreak of the Second World War, the hotel's room 305 was the unlikely scene of a brutal diamond heist. A gang of four public school boys, all 'from good homes', and afterwards dubbed 'the

◂ Standing at one hundred feet, it was the tallest building in London when it first opened in 1889, and against local objections, planning permission was granted because it was felt that the building would add to the 'architectural dignity' of the West End.

Top left: You are never short of something to read at Mandarin Oriental Hyde Park, London. Each room comes with a special selection of books handpicked by the Mayfair bookseller Heywood Hill.

Top right: In the Hyde Park Garden restaurant, guests are transported to a secluded, quintessentially British garden, situated in the Royal Park itself. Its menu, too, is inspired by British botanicals found in gardens all over the country.

Bottom: Every stay is enhanced by the sight and sounds of royal Household Cavalry horses parading by on the bridle paths of Hyde Park each morning.

Each of the suites, including those located in the turrets of the building with their circular interiors, are reminiscent of a luxury private apartment boasting floor-to-ceiling windows.

Mayfair playboys' in the press, had asked Étienne Bellenger, the manager of the London branch of Cartier, 'the king of jewellers and the jeweller of kings', to bring samples of diamond rings suitable for an engagement present to the hotel for them to inspect. The hotel's reputation and the men's evident rank, their expensive Savile Row tailored suits and old-school ties emblems of honour, ensured that this unusual request was obeyed without question. But no sooner had Bellenger opened his case then the men repeatedly coshed him over the head and made off with about £13,000 worth of jewellery – in today's money around half a million pounds. Their escape was short-lived. The gang, unable to dispose of their ill-gotten gains, were rounded up less than twenty-four hours later in Oxford, having already wasted valuable getaway time celebrating their robbery by trawling the pubs and nightclubs of Mayfair.

Nothing quite so unsavoury can really be imagined happening there now. The hotel was obviously considered safe enough for their Royal Highnesses William and Catherine, the current Prince and Princess of Wales, to celebrate their forthcoming wedding here in 2011, an event attended by 142 royals without incident.

It was quintessentially English novelist Evelyn Waugh, a regular guest for over twenty years, who once commended the hotel's 'civilised view' and the presence of the glorious park just beyond its windows, coupled with the sound of Household Cavalry horses clip-clopping by on the bridle paths outside each morning, that continues to make a stay in the present-day Mandarin Oriental Hyde Park, London, feel extra special.

In 2018, the hotel underwent a major renovation that saw its interiors updated by the award-wining designer Joyce Wang whose new scheme sought to bring the park inside. She created a bespoke wallpaper that mimicked the texture of tree bark; contemporary light fittings with shades in the shape of acorns replaced dowdier chandeliers and table decorations in the form of twigs became a motif of The Rosebery, where the hotel's unsurpassed afternoon tea is served. Such arboreal detailing is found in each of its 141 rooms and 40 suites, with bridleway patterning on the ceilings and walls. Meanwhile, each of its five distinguished Presidential Suites is named in honour of the park's great horticultural heroes, figures like the pioneering landscape architect and royal gardener Charles Bridgeman. Each suite comes with a specially curated library of books handpicked by the Mayfair bookseller Heywood Hill, whose one-time manager Handasyde Buchanan was the author of books on natural history and kept up a correspondence

Oilette
HYDE PARK HOTEL overlooking the Park.

HYDE PARK HOTEL,
LONDON
from the Serpentine.
A. BURKART & Co. Ltd. LONDON.

◂ A historical postcard and painting show various views of the famous London landmark. Top: The hotel's façade as seen from Hyde Park in 1905. Bottom: A view from the Serpentine, painted in 1914.

▴ Top: Since 1902, when it first opened as a hotel, the entrance to Mandarin Oriental Hyde Park, London, has been in fashionable Knightsbridge. Bottom left: The wartime prime minister, Winston Churchill, was a frequent guest to the hotel, pictured here in 1946. Bottom right: The British royal family also honors the hotel now and again for festive occasions. The late Queen Elizabeth II learnt to dance in the hotel's ballroom as a child. She is pictured here arriving for a party at the hotel on the eve of the royal wedding of the current Prince and Princess of Wales, William and Catherine, in 2011.

with Waugh, whose friend, the writer and socialite Nancy Mitford also worked for a time in the shop.

Fine dining has been overseen at Mandarin Oriental Hyde Park, London, by that master of English gastronomic wizardry Heston Blumenthal for well over a decade. Dinner by Heston Blumenthal, his two-Michelin-starred restaurant, not only mines British culinary history for gold with dishes such as spiced squab pigeon with artichokes and ale but also benefits from prime views of the park. Breakfast is served in the same dining room with serene greenery in sight, making it the ideal place to start your day.

Night owls, on the other hand, can avail themselves of The Aubrey restaurant, which offers not only mouthwatering contemporary interpretations of traditional Japanese Izakaya dishes but also seeks to give diners something of the taste of a good night out in Ginza with a range of signature drinks to accompany the food. At the weekend, it rolls out free flowing all-day brunches and there are DJ sets late into the night. A picture of this eatery's namesake, the aesthete artist Aubrey Beardsley, looking suitably fawn-like, not only hangs on the densely decorated black-lacquered wall of this diner but his illustrations also grace the cover of its cocktail menu, which pays homage to The Yellow Book, the infamous house journal of late-Victorian decadents. They would surely have fit in fine just here. Though for those who overindulge in the here and now, the best restoratives the twenty-first century has to offer are on hand in the hotel's state-of-the-art wellness and fitness centre on the lower ground floor.

◂ Top: With views of the bustle of Knightsbridge, The Rosebery is home to that most British of institutions, afternoon tea, as well as offering all day dining.

◂ Bottom: Chic interiors, its award-winning champagne cocktails and a dedicated caviar menu make Mandarin Bar one of London's most stylish nightspots.

▴ The bedroom of this Presidential Suite boasts custom-made furnishings and the fine views of the park.

LE BRISTOL PARIS

PARIS · FRANCE

The epitome of Parisian elegance and art de vivre – adored for its outstanding dining tradition, its lush 1,200 square metre courtyard garden and its charming rooftop swimming pool.

On 8 April 1975, the singer, dancer and civil rights activist Josephine Baker was honoured with a gala dinner for 250 people in the Salon Castellane of the hotel Le Bristol Paris to celebrate the fiftieth anniversary of her Paris debut at the Théâtre Bobino. The bash was attended by Princess Grace of Monaco, who helped the sixty-eight-year-old laureate cut a seven-tiered cake iced with spun sugar, and Mick Jagger of the Rolling Stones. A high time was had by all, and it was 4 a.m. before the festivities ended. Sadly the party was to prove Baker's swan song, as just two days later she suffered a stroke, fell into a coma and later died. But the hotel's present-day and suitably lavish seventh-floor Suite 1925, pays tribute to her memory; pictures of the star, including George Hoyningen-Huene's iconic monochrome photograph of Baker in her Jazz Age heyday, adorn its walls.

Baker famously was an animal lover and kept some rather unorthodox pets: a cheetah named Chiquita (once part of her stage-act), a goat called Toutoute, that had the run of her nightclub dressing room, and Albert the pig, were among the creatures that she doted on alongside a snake and numerous cats and dogs. And Le Bristol Paris, which opened its doors in the same year that Baker took to the stage at the Bobino, has been named as 'one of most pet-friendly hotels in world'. Indeed, canine and feline visitors can expect to be every bit as pampered as their human owners, the hotel laying on homemade treats, comfy pet beds and blankets, special bowls as well as dog walking and grooming services. Since 2021, Le Bristol Paris has also been blessed by the warm and welcoming presence of the pedigree Birman cat Socrate, the son of Fa-Raon, the hotel's previous and much-loved permanent feline resident. Fa-Raon's likeness, in naive portraits by amateur artists, decorated the interiors of Les Amis d'Hippolyte, the hotel's fun-filled children's clubroom.

The Hollywood actor-comedian W. C. Fields is said to have quipped 'never work with animals or children'. Le Bristol Paris caters for both attentively and has welcomed many a movie star, too, from Charlie Chaplin and Rita Hayworth in the silver screen era to more recent guests George Clooney and Woody Allen, who filmed scenes for his fantastical 2011 comedy *Midnight in Paris* in the hotel's Panoramic Suite.

At the quieter end of the Rue du Faubourg Saint-Honoré, with the Elysée Palace, international embassies and Paris's chicest boutiques, haute couture houses, landmark stores and high-end art galleries near at hand, Le Bristol Paris is as unashamedly grand as its *quartier,* with an imposing Comblanchien stone frontage, an epic marble foyer and fine antique furnishings and tapestries throughout. Yet there is nothing stuffy about it. The place exudes cosiness and a supreme kind of Gallic comfort – cue Louis XV wingback chairs – that never goes out of fashion.

The first hotel in the French capital to be awarded the appellation 'Palace', it was founded by Hippolyte Jammet, the son of a Parisian restaurateur, who named his establishment, emblematically, after the British aristocrat Frederick Augustus Hervey, 4th Earl of Bristol and Bishop of Cloyne and Derry. Hervey was a ceaseless traveller with exacting standards whose nod of approval was equivalent in the eighteenth century of the five-star rating that Le Bristol Paris itself holds today.

One of the few luxury hotels in Paris not to be requisitioned by the Nazis, it was used as the American Embassy during the Second World War. The hotel remained in the hands of the Jammet family until 1978, when it passed to its current owners and another dynasty, the Oetkers. The hotel takes it as a badge of honour that it not only remains a family-run concern but that it also continues to host heirs of the founding Jammet clan to this day.

With the rooftops of Paris and the Eiffel Tower within view from the hotel's balconies, Le Bristol Paris offers a window onto one the most romantic cities in the world.

◀ Invisible to passers-by on the street outside, the hotel's courtyard garden, Le Jardin Français (top), is a lush green oasis at the heart of the hotel and lined by the airy and art-adorned Colonnade (bottom left).

▲ A true Parisian pied-à-terre, the bow windows of the Suite Lumière surveys the Rue du Faubourg Saint-Honoré and invite an abundance of natural light to flood generous interiors that feature a library corridor.

Perhaps one of the hotel's most enchanting features is its courtyard garden, Le Jardin Français, an oasis of some 1,200 square metres of verdure recently replanted by the English landscape gardener Arabella Lennox-Boyd, where visitors can relax and take lunch, tea or enjoy a glass of wine. Another joy is the hotel's boat-shaped roof-top chlorine-free swimming pool, which can be reached in the hotel's elegant art deco lift or via its spiral stone staircase, and whose terraces offer unsurpassed views of Montmartre and the Eiffel Tower. Many guests, the hotel maintains, head to the roof to unwind after indulging in revitalizing sessions at Spa Le Bristol, where the La Prairie team supply a range of therapeutic and beauty treatments to nourish mind, body and spirit.

Sustenance of a more conventionally culinary sort meanwhile is found in Epicure, the hotel's aptly named and three-star Michelin in-house gourmet restaurant, its no less acclaimed newer brassiere 114 Faubourg, with one Michelin star, and Café Antonia, an all-day eatery with frescoed walls whose signature dish is a French green bean and Camus artichoke with hazelnuts salad. Though the sweet-toothed and less calorie-conscious have the deliciously decadent *chocolat chaud* as an option.

Another unique feature of the hotel, however, is that all of its freshly baked bread is made from grain milled on site as Le Bristol Paris houses the only hotel-based mill in Paris. They also produce their own honey as well as their own water utilizing a Swiss-designed filtering system, BE WTR, as an ecologically minded alternative to bottled water. All the hotel's restaurants and the bill of fare at Le Bar du Bristol, which hosts DJ-driven 'Bristol After Dark' parties for those – in the spirit of Josephine Baker – looking to make a night of it, come under the command of the hotel's executive chef, Arnaud Faye. A native of Auvergne, in rural central France, and a Meilleur Ouvrier de France (Best Craftsman in France), Faye has been credited with bringing a subtle contemporary twist to many a classic French dish and putting the issue of greater sustainability at the forefront of the hotel's food offerings.

All the time-honoured courtesies of a century-old institution remain, from handwritten personalized notes and tailor-made itineraries to the discreet service of its smartly liveried members of staff. But Le Bristol Paris has embraced the digital and in recent years launched 'Le Bristol Unlocked' its NFT collection. Although a Grande Dame, in many respects, Le Bristol Paris has the relaxed air and easy ambiance of, say, a newer boutique hotel, but with an august heritage that surely any such modern rival would die for.

With its wooden shelves decorated by antique silver and copperware and counters overflowing with provisions, from fine wines and jars of honey harvested from the hotel's own hives to beechwood-smoked salmon and game bird pie (and not forgetting the bread, freshly baked from flour milled on-site), L'Épicerie – or 'grocery' – is gourmet heaven, its fare specially prepared daily by a dedicated team of artisans.

◂ As grand as its quartier, the hotel's Comblanchien stone frontage (top) and its staircase (bottom) in days gone by. They still set the hotel's comfortingly classic tone today.

▸ The singer, dancer and civil rights activist Josephine Baker (seated) pictured here greeting the French actor Mireille Darc at the star-studded gala dinner held for her in the Salon Castellane of Le Bristol Paris on 8 April 1975.

LE BRISTOL
RESTAVRANT
PALACE

On the sixth floor, the Paris Suite (top left and right) offers breathtaking views of the city from its wraparound wrought-iron balcony, including the Eiffel Tower. The sumptuously furnished Imperial Suite (right) provides a haven for the discerning connoisseur. The fifth-floor Azur Terrace Suite (bottom left), meanwhile, comes with an immense flower-filled terrace and vibrant ceramic tiles by Agnès Sandahl.

The enchanting, nautical-themed rooftop swimming pool and outdoor sun deck (top left) on the sixth floor of the hotel is the ideal arena for those looking to exercise or merely to cool off and catch some rays. The sunlight-filled Spa Le Bristol offers a wealth of wellness and beauty treatments in its bespoke salons (bottom left and right). Afternoon tea or coffee (top right) may be enjoyed with colourful macarons and decadent tarts made by the hotel's pastry chefs, while overlooking the city (right), here with a view of the Grand Palais from the Paris Suite.

THE PENINSULA HONG KONG

HONG KONG · CHINA

The 'Grande Dame of the Far East',
The Peninsula Hong Kong continues to offer
a blend of the best of Eastern and Western
hospitality, setting hotel standards worldwide.

PHILIPS
HYUNDAI

HYUNDAI
SAMSUNG

As the American-born writer Henry James keenly observed in his great 1881 novel *The Portrait of a Lady*, 'There are few hours in life more agreeable than the hour dedicated to the ceremony known as afternoon tea.' And there are fewer places more agreeable to enjoy this ceremony than The Lobby of The Peninsula Hong Kong, which itself has often been described – and with good reason – as 'the most elegant meeting place in Hong Kong'. With its gilded plasterwork, columns and coffered ceilings, swish balconies and staircases, the two-storey lobby is a noble entranceway by any standards. The ritual of afternoon tea might be considered something of a hangover from colonial times. This, after all, was a repast popularized by the English upper crust in the early nineteenth century. Nevertheless, it was soon adopted by all classes across the Empire and considered such a mainstay of British life that 'teatime' was celebrated in the lyrics of a popular comic song of the 1930s, which maintained that 'when the clock strikes four, everything stops for tea.' While, sadly, the habit has largely died out in England, it not only lives on in Hong Kong at The Peninsula Hong Kong, but afternoon tea has also become a revered local tradition in its own right.

On marble-topped tables, silver pots of Indian, Earl Grey or Jasmine tea are proffered and the drink served in eggshell-thin bone china cups with saucers. Rounds of delicate savoury finger sandwiches, their crusts cut off and filled variously with smoked salmon, cucumber, chicken, prawns and egg salad are followed by buttery scones, baked to a recipe unchanged in half a century and lavished with homemade strawberry jam and clotted cream. The whole thing, an exercise in refined indulgence of the best kind, is enjoyed to the polite strains of a live band playing jazz and classical standards.

Affectionately known as 'The Pen', the hotel first opened its doors in 1928. Its founder was Ellis 'Elly' Kadoorie, a Jewish merchant from Baghdad who had established a successful brokering house and whose interests in Hong Kong included the main energy company, China Light and Power. Kadoorie, whose descendants are still represented on The Peninsula's board, aspired to create 'the finest hotel east of Suez'. Palmer and Turner, the architectural firm responsible for the offices of the Hongkong and Shanghai Banking Corporation (HSBC) in both Hong Kong and on the Bund in Shanghai, and later the Peace Hotel on the same waterfront, produced a building in the ornate Renaissance and Baroque Revival styles that at seven storeys in height was then the tallest building in the Far East.

Locations can make or break hotels, and The Pen, situated in Salisbury Road, Tsim Sha Tsui, was ideally placed for international visitors arriving either by boat on the ocean liners that disembarked on the nearby Kowloon quayside or by train, the neighbouring station being the final stop for European passengers on the Trans-Siberian Railway. It thrived accordingly. Prince Henry, Duke of Gloucester, checked in within a year of its opening and this aristocratic seal of approval helped to ensure it attracted a distinguished clientele ever afterwards. The Hollywood actor-director Charlie Chaplin is just one of the starry names who have signed the guest book. He stayed at The Pen while filming 'A Countess from Hong Kong' in 1967 and is said to have barely ventured beyond its doors during his entire time in Hong Kong, which may be taken as a tribute to the service he received here.

Visitors are still well served today by transport options: a Hong Kong Mass Transit Railway station, which connects guests with a high-speed network that extends to and from mainland China, is less than a minute's walk away; the Star Ferry Pier is around five minutes away; and both the Kai Tak Cruise terminal and the Chek Lap Kok International Airport can be reached by car in around thirty minutes. The hotel itself also keeps a

◀ **Interiors combine classical grandeur with timeless modern elegance.**

▶ **The Pen's fleet of custom-made Rolls-Royce limousines is among the hotel's most charming features.**

THE PENINSULA
THE PENINSULA
MP 3128

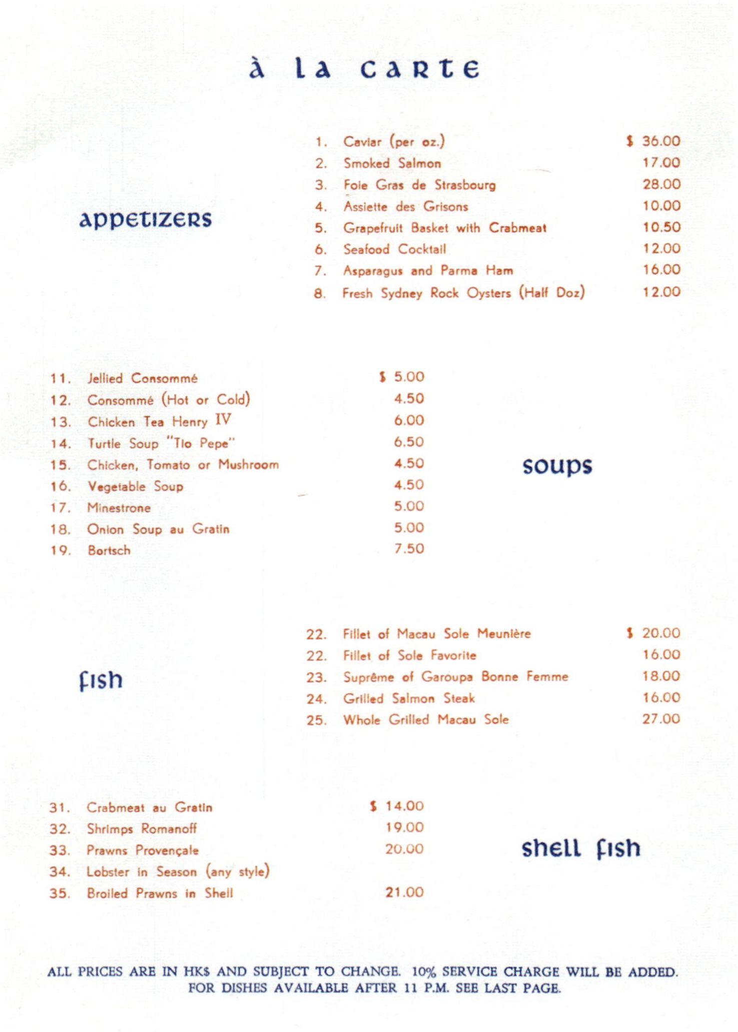

à la carte

appetizers

1.	Caviar (per oz.)	$ 36.00
2.	Smoked Salmon	17.00
3.	Foie Gras de Strasbourg	28.00
4.	Assiette des Grisons	10.00
5.	Grapefruit Basket with Crabmeat	10.50
6.	Seafood Cocktail	12.00
7.	Asparagus and Parma Ham	16.00
8.	Fresh Sydney Rock Oysters (Half Doz)	12.00

soups

11.	Jellied Consommé	$ 5.00
12.	Consommé (Hot or Cold)	4.50
13.	Chicken Tea Henry IV	6.00
14.	Turtle Soup "Tio Pepe"	6.50
15.	Chicken, Tomato or Mushroom	4.50
16.	Vegetable Soup	4.50
17.	Minestrone	5.00
18.	Onion Soup au Gratin	5.00
19.	Bortsch	7.50

fish

22.	Fillet of Macau Sole Meunière	$ 20.00
22.	Fillet of Sole Favorite	16.00
23.	Suprême of Garoupa Bonne Femme	18.00
24.	Grilled Salmon Steak	16.00
25.	Whole Grilled Macau Sole	27.00

shell fish

31.	Crabmeat au Gratin	$ 14.00
32.	Shrimps Romanoff	19.00
33.	Prawns Provençale	20.00
34.	Lobster in Season (any style)	
35.	Broiled Prawns in Shell	21.00

ALL PRICES ARE IN HK$ AND SUBJECT TO CHANGE. 10% SERVICE CHARGE WILL BE ADDED.
FOR DISHES AVAILABLE AFTER 11 P.M. SEE LAST PAGE.

Fine dining in glorious surroundings have always been a recipe for success here.

The family atmosphere at The Pen extends to staff, pictured here with their own children.

A display of vintage memorabilia paints a picture of the hotel in days gone by.

Tradition is vitally important here but so is moving with the times. Pictured here is one of the hotel's vintage Rolls-Royces. The modern Rolls-Royce fleet of The Peninsula Hong Kong now come with Wi-Fi and the latest touchscreen tech.

fleet of custom-made Rolls-Royce limousines, liveried in a distinctive and distinguished racing Peninsula green, at its guests' disposal. This service, like the afternoon tea, is another of The Pen's delightfully old-school perks.

Nevertheless, the hotel is, in many other respects, as up to date as any other. Even the Rolls-Royces come with Wi-Fi, touchscreen tech and in-car passenger home cinema viewing screens with high spec-sound systems. The oldest rooms are fitted with triple-glazed soundproof windows that enhance the sense of cocooned comfort, and all mod cons installed are resolutely of the era of TikTok and X. More recent refits have also ensured that the hotel's furnishings and artworks, if never forgetting the past and celebrating such local artisanal crafts as Chinese ink brush painting and stonemasonry, feel similarly part of the twenty-first century, and a good example of luxury 2.0, if you will. Its present managing director, Joseph W. Y. Chong, joined The Peninsula Beijing in 2000 and after a spell as Resident Manager at The Peninsula Bangkok oversaw the reopening of The Peninsula Shanghai and so has witnessed the rapid shifts in tourism in this region since the start of the millennium first hand.

The Pen's pathway to modernization already began in 1994. The hotel was then extended with an adjacent thirty-storey tower replete with a heliport, an additional 130 guest rooms and a swimming pool and a spa designed by Orlando Diaz-Azcuy. The new structure also benefits from unimpeded views of Hong Kong Island and Victoria Harbour to the south and the city centre and mountain range to the North. Some of the best views are to be had in Felix, the hotel's most exciting restaurant on the 28th floor: its avant-garde decor, fittings, fixtures and tableware are all the work of the gloriously unconventional French designer and industrial architect Philippe Starck. Named after Felix Bieger, one of the hotel's longest serving managers, the restaurant is a feast for the eyes as much as for the stomach. Its dishes provide a winning spin on modern European cuisine with the emphasis on fresh ingredients, simple preparation and healthy dining. Another of The Pen's esteemed eateries, the more august and Michelin-starred Gaddi's, established in 1953, also takes its name from another former directors. Leo Gaddi was the hotel's first general manager and a man who helped to restore the hotel to its former glory after its ravaging by occupying Japanese forces during the Second World War. Indeed, Hong Kong's British governor Sir Mark Young had surrendered to the Japanese in 1941 at the end of the Battle of Hong Kong in the hotel.

A gastronomic destination now for generations of visitors to, and residents of, Hong Kong, Gaddi's specializes in fine French cuisine with an impeccable wine list to match and all served beneath crystal chandeliers and with glistening antique silverware in a salon-style setting. Its kitchen and cellars are currently presided over by Anne Sophie-Nicolas, the restaurant's first female Chef de Cuisine, whose astutely contemporary take on classic Gallic cooking is reflected in the menus daily. Authentic Cantonese cuisine is the order of the day in the much-lauded Spring Moon restaurant, while the Alpine cabin themed Chesa is one of only two Swiss restaurants in the whole of Hong Kong and widely held to be the best, its fondue and raclette earning high praise among those in the know. Indeed, the hotel once supplied the catering service for all Swissair flights from Hong Kong to Zurich, and the idea for the Chesa restaurant initially grew from a successful promotional menu specializing in Swiss national delicacies devised for the airline in 1963.

Many returning visitors, however, retain a particular soft spot for The Verandah. This first-floor quality buffet diner originally opened in 1933 is a place to sit in splendour and indulge in a lazy breakfast, a light lunch, afternoon cake and coffee, a laid-back evening meal or all four over the course of a day. No one would bat an eyelid if you did. The guest is king here – and treated like one, too.

◄ **The time-honoured ritual of taking tea continues to reign supreme. Here, beyond the afternoon tea of The Pen, a tea has been prepared as part of a spa treatment.**

◀ Originally opened in 1933, The Verandah fine dining buffet offers a wide variety of gastronomic delights throughout the day.

The elegant dining room, graced by art deco stained-glass windows, of the Michelin-starred Spring Moon, one of Hong Kong's most celebrated Cantonese restaurants.

With its sky-high harbour views and sleek, modern Philippe Starck-designed interiors, Felix makes for a visually arresting dining experience.

▶ Set high in the upper floors of The Peninsula Tower, The Peninsula Suite, the hotel's presidential suite, offers dazzling panoramic vistas of the Victoria Harbour and Hong Kong Island.

THE PIERRE NY

NEW YORK CITY · UNITED STATES

Ever since the hotel opened in 1930, it has been revered as both a quintessential monument to New York City grandeur and an outstanding archetype of service excellence.

On the corner of East 61st Street and Fifth Avenue, The Pierre NY, a Taj Hotel, stands facing Central Park. A unique building, modelled after the Royal Chapel at the Palace of Versailles, it exudes a certain French Gothic glamour but is unmistakably a product of the American Jazz Age and is all the classier for it.

Door staff are often described as the public face of a hotel. But in the case of John Foley, the genuinely legendary doorman of The Pierre NY, a Taj Hotel, for some fifty-four years, this was more true than usual. For Foley appeared in numerous fashion photoshoots, perhaps most memorably in an iconic spread for *Vogue* magazine by Oliviero Toscani in 1974; the diminutive doorman, spruce in his peaked cap and immaculately pressed uniform, was pictured flanked by statuesque models outside the hotel's entrance on East 61st Street. But then fashion and The Pierre NY have long gone hand in hand. The trendsetting Coco Chanel, famous for her namesake No. 5 scent and making the little black dress a wardrobe staple, stayed here on her first trip to New York in 1932. Thirty years later, Yves Saint Laurent chose the hotel as the venue to stage his debut collection in America. In 1976, he took possession of apartment #3804, this property afterwards passing into the hands of the Valentino fashion house co-founder Giancarlo Giammetti and more recently the German designer Tomas Maier. His compatriot Karl Lagerfeld, who made The Pierre NY his base whenever in New York, was said to measure any distance in the city by how far it was from the hotel. And why not? The hotel's location is another of its assets, standing as it does forty-one storeys high on the corner of East 61st Street and Fifth Avenue and directly opposite Central Park.

The Pierre NY has been said to look more like a stately French château than your typical New York hotel, and its exterior was designated a historic landmark by the New York City Landmarks Preservation Commission back in 1981. As a matter of fact, its upper floors, topped by a steep copper roof, were consciously modelled on the Royal Chapel by Jules Hardouin-Mansart at the Palace of Versailles, the royal residence of King Louis XIV of pre-Revolutionary France. The hotel's visionary founder, Charles Pierre Casalasco was also French. He originally hailed from Ajaccio in Corsica, the birthplace of Napoleon Bonaparte. The son of a restaurateur, Charles Pierre toiled in his father's establishment until turning eighteen when he left Corsica for good, heading first to Monte Carlo on the French Riviera. Once there (and ever afterward known simply as Charles Pierre), he obtained a post as a pageboy at the Hôtel Anglais in 1897. Monte Carlo was then in the gilded heyday of the Belle Époque. The resort, initially established by affluent, if ailing, members of the British aristocracy fleeing cold, damp winters at home, was knee deep in monarchs, viscounts, duchesses and monied industrialists. Charles Pierre was to serve them all, soaking up everything he could learn about the exacting demands of the blue blooded and wealthy in the process.

Charles Pierre subsequently headed to Paris, immersing himself in that city's fine dining scene. His talent in this area was spotted by Louis Sherry, and in 1904, Charles Pierre crossed the Atlantic for New York to work in the American-born hotelier and restauranteur's eponymous eatery on 44th Street and Fifth Avenue. Sherry's catered to Manhattan's elite, counting the financier J. P. Morgan and the wealthy lawyer, politician and social reformer Elbridge Thomas Gerry among its diners. After a twelve-year stint, Charles Pierre moved on, allegedly falling out with Sherry over his refusal to allow women to smoke in the restaurant. Following a brief turn at the old Ritz-Carlton Hotel at 46th and Madison, he set up his own restaurant, first at 11 East 45th Street before settling on more distinguished premises at 230 Park Avenue, where debutante dinners proved a meal ticket.

But it was the death in 1927 of his former loyal Sherry's patron, Elbridge Thomas Gerry, that allowed him to realize the dream of opening a hotel. Gerry's lavish Fifth Avenue mansion in the French Renaissance

From mid-March into early May, the Yoshino and Kwanzan cherry trees in nearby Central Park come into bloom, only adding to the pleasure of a springtime stay at The Pierre NY.

style, already fighting a losing battle on the Upper East Side skyline against a rising tide of art-deco skyscrapers, was inherited by his son Robert. He, alongside Otto Hahn and Walter Chrysler, was to become one of the major financial backers of Charles Pierre's scheme to have it promptly torn down and replaced by a new high-rise hotel.

The Pierre NY was designed by Schultze and Weaver, the architectural firm responsible for several other significant hotels in the city, not least the nearby Sherry-Netherland Hotel. Auguste Escoffier, the French culinary master acclaimed as the 'king of chefs and chef of kings' was brought in to advise on the kitchen and menu. His input was invaluable and endures still at The Pierre's in-house restaurant, Perrine. Yet with slightly unpropitious timing, the hotel was to open its doors, and at a cost of $15 million dollars, on 1 October 1930, close to a year after the Wall Street Crash. With prohibition in place until 1933, its ending eventually celebrated in suitably champagne-soaked fashion with the opening of a new supper club and the introduction of evenings of lively big band entertainment, the hotel endured a rocky few years. Its future would not be assured until it was acquired by J. Paul Getty in 1938, the oil magnate and then richest man in the world, who joked that it was his 'only asset above ground'.

Under Getty's watch, the ballroom was doubled in size and both the Cotillion Room and the popular Cafe Pierre cocktail bar and restaurant were opened. The ballroom of the former was to be immortalized on film in the famous tango scene in the 1992 movie *Scent of a Woman*, for which Al Pacino won the Academy Award for Best Actor. Such was Cafe Pierre's acclaim meanwhile in the post-prohibition era that its 'Maître de Bar' Oscar Haimo began publishing an annual newsletter celebrating its intoxicating offerings. The Oval Room was remade into The Rotunda, with its arresting central staircase and its walls later adorned by Edward Melcarth's iconic trompe l'oeil murals. There, the Birdcage, the world's first hanging glass cocktail lounge was a favourite backdrop for fashion shoots by luxury brands, such as Brioni, until it was removed in the late 1960s. Those seeking the taste of South Asia, could enjoy Indian curries from the Pierre Grill, and although the grill no longer exists, Indian dishes remain cherished fixtures of the modern-day menu of Perrine. But perhaps the greatest change Getty made came in the late 1950s when he decided to convert some of the hotel's suites into luxurious co-op apartments. The co-op owners and others were to buy the building, while Getty and Co were left to run the hotel. While the hotel has since passed through various hands including the Trust House Forte and Four Seasons groups, that arrangement holds good today. There are eighty

◂ A room with a view, many of The Pierre's suites provide similarly breathtaking vistas of the Big Apple.

▴ The Pierre arose in the dawn of the skyscraper, and its striking profile, photographed here in the 1930s, has remained a Manhattan landmark ever since.

co-op apartments, whose present occupants range from the former Walt Disney CEO, Michael Eisner, to the fashion entrepreneur Tory Burch. Meanwhile, The Pierre's current lessee and operator Taj Hotels looks after the 189 hotel rooms and suites, including the palatial six-bedroom, seven-bathroom Presidential Suite.

Functions, though, have been central to the hotel's business plan with debutante balls and society wedding parties among its specialties from the very outset. Symbolically, more recently, Vera Wang, the elite figure skater and *Vogue* magazine editor turned bridal gown designer to such celebrities as Kim Kardashian, Chelsea Clinton and Ariana Grande, herself got married in the hotel in 1989. But such events do more than just make money, they serve to bind The Pierre NY to the fabric of New York life: its balls, parties and galas the talk of the town for several generations of the city's inhabitants.

The hotel's enforced closure during the Covid-19 pandemic in 2020 and the subsequent limits placed on the size of social gatherings in the immediate wake were keenly felt. But The Pierre NY embarked on an ambitious $20 million renovation plan overseen by Michael S. Smith, the former interior designer to President Barack Obama at the White House. In 2022, following the redesign of the interdisciplinary architectural firm Sawyer | Berson, the Grand Ballroom reopened, reborn nearly a century after it first opened and looking lovelier than ever.

As with any great hotel it is the staff who make all the difference, and at The Pierre NY close to eighty handpicked employees might work a single event. The over thirty attending to the guests' every need as dedicated banquet servers ensure flawless five-star service every time. Each year the hotel presents a highly coveted prize for the most outstanding employee: the Foley Award, named, of course, in honour of that much photographed doorman, John Foley. A man whose service and style summed up the whole ethos of The Pierre NY for more than half a century and whose spirit continues to guide its actions today.

The gilded doorway of The Pierre NY, its arresting main entrance sets the tone of high-class luxury inside.

▶ These two suites named, respectively, in honour of Jamsetji Tata, founder of the Taj Group who currently operates the hotel, and the French chef Auguste Escoffier, who oversaw its opening menus, similarly combine the best of the old and new in their refined decor.

◀ The fashion designer Yves Saint Laurent launched his debut New York collection at The Pierre NY and is pictured here at the hotel with the model and actor Lois Chiles in 1974.

▲ The hotel has long been a haunt of the fashionable and famous, clockwise: Coco Chanel, Andy Warhol, Elizabeth Taylor with husband Eddie Fisher (middle), Barbra Streisand and Valentino, Gigi Hadid, Bruna Marquezine and Janelle Monáe.

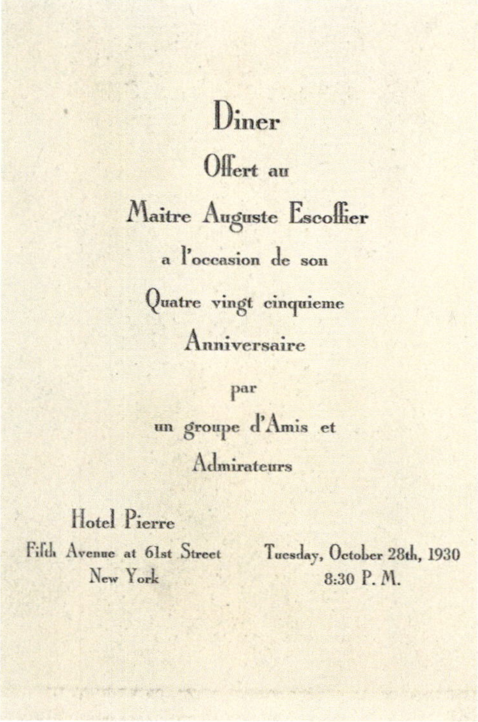
Diner
Offert au
Maitre Auguste Escoffier
a l'occasion de son
Quatre vingt cinquieme
Anniversaire
par
un groupe d'Amis et
Admirateurs

Hotel Pierre
Fifth Avenue at 61st Street
New York

Tuesday, October 28th, 1930
8:30 P. M.

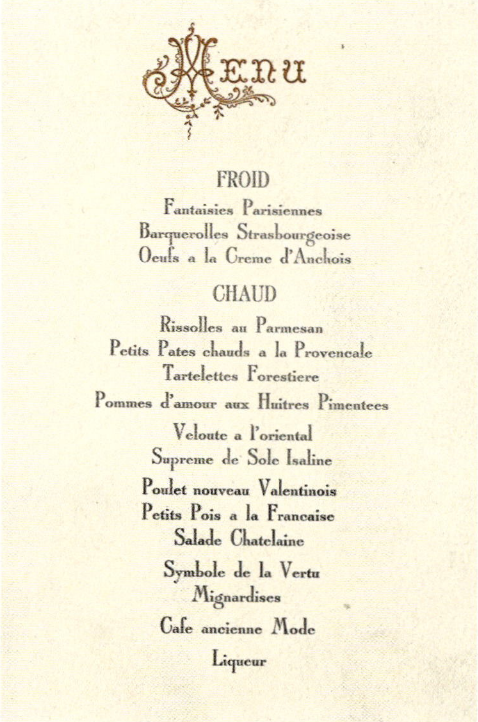
Menu

FROID
Fantaisies Parisiennes
Barquerolles Strasbourgeoise
Oeufs a la Creme d'Anchois

CHAUD
Rissolles au Parmesan
Petits Pates chauds a la Provencale
Tartelettes Forestiere
Pommes d'amour aux Huitres Pimentees
Veloute a l'oriental
Supreme de Sole Isaline
Poulet nouveau Valentinois
Petits Pois a la Francaise
Salade Chatelaine
Symbole de la Vertu
Mignardises
Cafe ancienne Mode
Liqueur

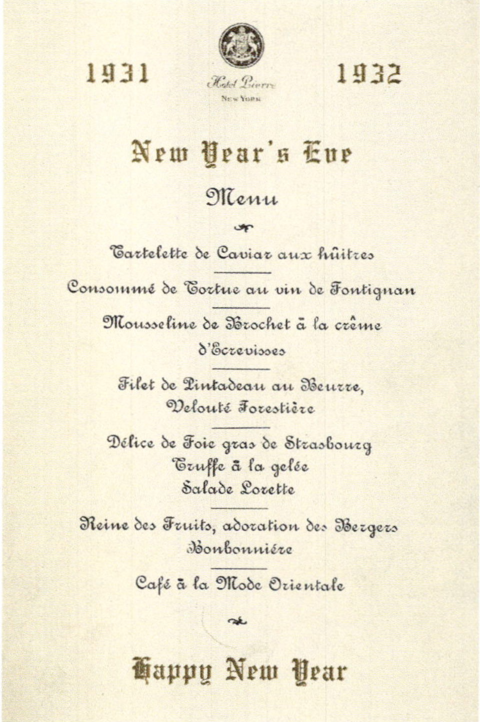
1931 Hotel Pierre New York 1932

New Year's Eve
Menu

Tartelette de Caviar aux hûitres
Consommé de Tortue au vin de Fontignan
Mousseline de Brochet ā la crême d'Ecrevisses
Filet de Pintadeau au Beurre, Velouté Forestière
Délice de Foie gras de Strasbourg
Truffe ā la gelée
Salade Lorette
Reine des Fruits, adoration des Bergers
Bonbonniére
Café ā la Mode Orientale

Happy New Year

Press adverts for the hotel from the 1930s boasted of 'Dinner and Supper Dancing on the Roof' for the winter debutante season and promised apartments tailored to guests' needs. Menus from the same period, meanwhile, reveal the bill of fare prepared to mark the French chef Auguste Escoffier's birthdays and New Year's Eve 1931.

▸ The Rotunda with its majestic staircase and the trompe l'oeil murals by Edward Melcarth and, below, the Grand Ballroom dressed to perfection for a wedding.

The expansive terrace of a Luxury Suite overlooks Central Park and Manhattan's Upper East Side.

VILLA LA MASSA

FLORENCE · ITALY

Dating from the thirteenth century, Villa la Massa was built as a country retreat for a leading Florentine family and remained in the hands of European aristocrats for the next six centuries until it was transformed into one of Italy's finest luxury hotels.

Politics in Renaissance Florence was never anything less than Machiavellian, and so it was that most of the leading aristocratic families of the era possessed estates in the Tuscan countryside. These were rustic retreats where the great and the good (or not so good, depending on your allegiances) might escape from the not infrequently plague-ridden city or courtly and papal intrigue for their health, safety and sanity, and to plot their next wily stratagem. Amid the agrarian beauty of olive groves, rolling hills and vineyards, with the scent of lemon and cypress trees in the air, and the tranquil cool blue waters of the River Arno nearby working their magic, too, thoughts could come into focus. And a fatal stabbing or a poisoning could be evaded, for a while at least.

Villa la Massa was just such a property. Lying in idyllic seclusion some fifteen minutes by car outside Florence and in the heart of the Chianti wine region, the original house was built in the thirteenth century as a summer bolthole for a leading Florentine family. It was to remain in the hands of a series of eminent aristocrats, many of whom added a tower or four here, or a fresco and chapel there, in accordance with the fashions of their respective days, until the late 1940s. After which, it was eventually converted into a hotel by its then less blue-blooded owners, the American Sears family of department store fame, in 1953.

The current hotel, extensively renovated within the last few years and a Five Star establishment, nevertheless continues to retain its aristocratic aura and wears its rich (in every sense of the word) Renaissance history and much else with pride. Spread over six separate classic Tuscan villas and set in twenty-five acres of beautifully lush parkland – its centrepiece a traditional Iris Garden (the flower is the emblem of the region) – there are fifty-one rooms (doubles and suites) along with three private apartments. None of which would shame a duke or duchess, the accommodations come in a range of shapes and sizes and decorative flavours: from the magnificently antique with four-poster beds, plush furnishings and frescos, to the more modern, utilizing local Tuscan handicrafts and earthy colour-schemes to create rooms that combine contemporary comfort with rural simplicity.

Villa la Massa boasts two main restaurants, Il Verrocchio and L'Oliveto Bistrot. The former is blessed with a terrace overlooking the River Arno, Tuscany's most vital and nourishing natural resource. While the gentle slopes of the Chianti Hills can be admired from the windows of its handsome dining room. Back in 1992, David Bowie chose to hold his post-ceremony wedding dinner here. Bono and Yoko Ono were among the celebrities who attended to celebrate what would prove to be his happy and long-lasting union with the model Iman. Wedding parties continue to be regular patrons; what was good enough for David Bowie can hardly be gainsaid, after all.

The present restaurant sources many of its fruits from its kitchen gardens, and its olive oil is drawn directly from its own groves. Regional Italian and gourmet Mediterranean dishes are its stock in trade, though there is nothing formulaic about the food – their turbot in a champagne sauce a much-cited favourite among returning visitors.

More relaxed luncheons may be found at L'Oliveto Bistrot, which by day serves up light meals and delicious pizza on its patio and is transformed into a charming Tuscan taverna by night. Both restaurants are managed by Chef Stefano Ballarino, who also teaches cookery masterclasses for guests, young and old, wishing to improve their culinary arts. Mixology lessons in cocktail-making, can be acquired in the Bar Mediceo, where expert staff will pour you the perfect glass of whatever you fancy and al fresco drinks alongside the Arno can be savoured in the most enchanting of surroundings.

Comprising six classic Tuscan villas, Villa la Massa lies in the heart of Tuscany's Chianti wine region.

▲ With interiors reflecting the hotel's aristocratic and Renaissance heritage, and a quiet secluded countryside location, Villa la Massa has the perfect mix of the regal and the rustic.

▶ Al fresco dining, with the scent of lemon and cypress trees in the air, is a pleasure all its own.

The hotel's cavernous wine cellar is not only well-stocked with the finest vintages and the perfect local Tuscan varieties (Chianti, Brunello di Montalcino, Vino Nobile di Montepulciano), it also dates from the fifteenth century and can be hired as a suitably atmospheric venue for a private dinner or intimate wine tasting party.

Meanwhile, Villa la Massa's wellness area, the Arno Spa, is housed within the former cellars of the villa and includes with treatment rooms, relaxation areas and a sauna and Roman bath, with a jacuzzi alongside a gym among its facilities. While a heated open-air swimming pool framed by loungers and a carpet of green lawns offers the chance to bathe above ground beneath cloudless blue skies. In the summer months, a poolside bar is open to provide drinks and snacks.

Both the so-called father of the Renaissance, the painter Giotto, and one of its greatest masters, Michelangelo, were born and worked in Tuscany, and the phenomenally wealthy ruling Medici family were the foremost patrons of the arts in Florence in that era: Filippo Brunelleschi, who was to provide the Florentine Cathedral with its dome – the largest masonry dome ever built and a structural, architectural and aesthetic marvel – was one of the recipients of their largess. Tuscany and Florence remain a Mecca for artists and art lovers of all stripes, and the Villa la Massa caters for those wishing to emulate the Florentine masters with drawing and painting sessions in its gardens with professional tutors. The picturesque buildings and grounds of the hotel proving suitably inspiring subjects that often brings out the best in many of these aspiring artists' work.

Top: Swim surrounded by the brilliant green lawns of the hotel's twenty-five-acre parkland. Bottom: Even inside the sumptuously furnished suites, a glimpse of the Tuscan countryside is never far away.

Breakfast on a balcony overlooking Villa la Massa's parkland or make a night of it inside by candlelight amid the finest of Florentine furnishings.

ROYAL PALM BEACHCOMBER LUXURY

MAURITIUS

With the highest standards of hospitality
in a location straight from a dream,
the Royal Palm Beachcomber Luxury combines
the greatest comfort with eco-responsibility.

Nicknamed 'Royal Calm' by many of its more waggish fans, the Royal Palm Beachcomber Luxury Hotel first opened in 1985 and was the first hotel in the Indian Ocean to be invited to join that most prestigious of associations, the Leading Hotels of the World. Luxury is found here in the art of perfecting the smallest details. What might seem like a minor touch – assigning each guest, upon arrival, their own dedicated sun lounger for the duration of their stay – speaks volumes about the level of care. Likewise, a glass of wine ordered comes, as one long-term guest noted approvingly, with a complimentary side of olives and homemade chocolate. Such little gestures matter and are often cited by frequent guests among their many reasons for returning.

Lying on the north-western tip of the island paradise of Mauritius on the Grand Sable – a sheltered, private sandy cove, not far from the vibrant beach-bar lined village of Grand Baie – its location is hard to beat. It is a setting of such tranquil beauty, where kicking back feels second nature, and that feeling is only enhanced by the hotel's fixtures. With three pools and plenty of decking and a beachfront of white sands, gently lapped by the ocean's emerald waves, and lined by giant Royal Palm trees, there is an abundance of thatched roofs, canopies and parasols offering shade and banks of pillowed seating areas and couches that outdo themselves in comfy plumpness.

In 2023, its famed sunken retro-style lounge bar, where cocktails and aperitifs can be taken with the most magnificent panoramic views of the bay, along with all of its 69 sea-facing suites, were part of a general revamp of the whole estate. Yet the updated mix of colour schemes inspired by the local environment and natural woods, gold-veined marble and travertine tiling across its interior decor, and the patterned screens, richly woven silks and airy linens of its fabrics and furnishings, has helped smarten it up without tarnishing any of its old charm. Its comparatively limited number of suites, and therefore guests, has always made it feel both select and high-end cosy. It is little wonder then that several heads of state and many celebrities are said to be regular visitors, cherishing its location in sunny seclusion and the quality of its service.

But every guest knows, the staff is the real heart and soul of this operation, something that is underlined by a wall display of 30 artful black-and-white photographs of the Royal Palm team at work. The pictures rather touchingly connect 'the ladies and gentlemen serving ladies and gentlemen', to quote the legendary Ritz-Carlton founder Horst H. Schulze. Every guest's daily needs are met by a dedicated band of staff known as 'Artisans', many of whom have been at the hotel for numerous years. These Artisans draw up specially individualized itineraries to ensure residents get the most out of their stay; and a whole range of excursions and activities, from glass-bottomed boat trips, kayaking and paddleboarding to martial arts instruction, can be arranged with them.

The latter courses are offered in the gym of the hotel's newly expanded wellness centre and spa, which is now fitted with the most technologically advanced equipment and offers exclusive treatments from the Swiss Valmont brand along with healing sessions with a Reiki master. You can even round off your day with vinyasa yoga at sunset.

The newest addition to the Royal Palm's restaurants is Grand Sable, a novel al fresco eatery on the beachfront that opened in October 2024. Offering a taste of the Mediterranean by the Indian Ocean, this restaurant's menu is regularly augmented by contributions from some of the world's leading chefs. In collaboration with the hotel's head chef, William Girard, the likes of the acclaimed French-Lebanese chef Alan Geaam and Charley Bouhier of Lyon's celebrated Lily of the Valley restaurant, have devised seasonal pop-up menus

◂ **Lying on the north-western tip of an island paradise in a sheltered, private sandy cove, the Royal Palm embodies the very essence of Mauritian hospitality, where every moment becomes an unforgettable memory.**

The hotel's immaculate beachfront offers guests a chance to dine barefoot on the sand beneath the stars.

for Grand Sable, making its bill of fare, rather delightfully, a constantly changing one.

If Grand Sable is something of a moveable feast, the hotel's Royal Grill is a sacrosanct weekly institution. This barefoot beach barbecue is held in grand style without fail every Thursday evening and is not to be missed. Neither is breakfast at La Goélette – the hotel's ocean-facing fine dining restaurant in the evening, where grilled fish and shellfish from the lagoon, Wagyu beef, ibérico pork and rare yellowfin tuna with Cajun spices are highlights of the nighttime menu. But it is also worth visiting first thing in the morning, not only for the superb cold buffet breakfast spreads and à la carte hot-cooked staples (think Eggs Benedict), but to catch a glimpse of sea turtles and seabirds on the sun-kissed waves.

Restaurant La Plage, meanwhile, an eatery and bar located on the beach beneath a majestic *Badamier* tree, is as good a spot as any for a lazy, grazing lunch of Creole-style shrimp salad, say, washed down with a chilled glass of rosé, or more casual dining later on. Pan-Asian cuisine and sushi, the latter overseen by the Mauritian sushi and sashimi master Chef Teka, are the preserve of the Asiya Restaurant on the lagoon.

The Beachcomber group, which operates a total of eight hotels in Mauritius (including the Royal Palm), along with one in the Seychelles and another in Morocco, has long been at the forefront of sustainable tourism. In 2024, the group received the Gold Award from EarthCheck for its sustainability initiatives, recognizing its 52 cast-iron commitments to preserving the environment. This builds on their earliest vision – as far back as 1999, they had already established the Fondation Espoir Développement Beachcomber (FED) to support socially disadvantaged Mauritians through various local projects. Such initiatives are particularly vital for small island nations like Mauritius, where tourism accounts for a fifth of the island's gross domestic product and where climate change and rising sea levels pose increasing challenges to coastal preservation. As one of Beachcomber's flagship properties, Royal Palm embodies this commitment, ensuring its paradise setting endures for future generations.

◂ The lounge with its well-stocked library is a great place to relax and catch up on some reading.

▴ The Presidential Suite, with its double-doors and terrace, affords breathtaking views of the beach, combining elegance with simplicity.

▸ Centred on a free-flowing, cascading pool, the spa and wellness centre offers a tranquil sanctuary for quiet relaxation and pampering.

◂ The hotel's loyal team seek to make guests feel that the Royal Palm is a true 'home from home'; many of its Artisans have over three decades of dedicated service.

Bottom left: Meals are presented 'service à la cloche' by its immaculately turned out Artisans, adding a touch of timeless sophistication to the ocean-side dining experience.

Bottom right: Sample a Medicament Royal, the hotel's signature drink, while revelling in the most magnificent views of the bay in sight.

ÇIRAĞAN PALACE

ISTANBUL · TÜRKİYE

First built by a seventeenth-century sultan as a gift for his daughter, Çırağan Palace Kempinski offers regal hospitality on Istanbul's historic waterfront where the East gloriously meets the West.

Once an imperial palace on the Bosphorus, Çırağan Palace Kempinski Istanbul had many lives before becoming a first-class hotel in 1990s. It once served as a seat for the royal court, a parliamentary chamber and then as a venue for beauty pageants, musical concerts and sporting contests.

Paradise, or *Jannah*, in the Islamic tradition is a garden, and in Persian the word itself is interchangeable. The lengthy history of the Çırağan Palace Hotel is storied and varied, intermingling with that of Istanbul. Its origins can be traced back to a time in the seventeenth century when an imperial garden, or *hasbahçe*, was laid out in what was then Constantinople, on the banks of the Bosphorus, the strait that connects the Black Sea to the Sea of Marmara, and from there to the Aegean and Mediterranean. Impeccably manicured, the Kazancıoğlu Gardens were for the exclusive use of Sultan Ahmed I and his family. A hundred years later, the Grand Vizier Ibrahim Pasha, the son-in-law of the then Sultan, Ahmed III, built a house for his wife Fatma in those grounds. This property became known as the 'Çırağan' Palace, a title that roughly translates as the 'Torch-Lit' or 'Light-Filled' Palace and derived from the lanterns, which illuminated the seasonal festivals that were held there to celebrate the blossoming multi-coloured tulips in the gardens. If more familiarly associated with the Dutch, tulips are native to Türkiye and so revered that their form has been incorporated as a motif on tiles in mosques and palaces across the Ottoman Empire. The flowers were part of annual rituals for centuries before they took Europe, especially the Low Countries, by storm.

Successive sultans were to build ever more lavish Çırağan Palaces on the same site – few of them, alas, living long enough to see their dream creations realized – until the last and grandest of all, at a cost of some 2.5 million gold coins, was completed in 1871 in the reign of Sultan Abdülaziz, to a design by the Baylans, a family of architects of Armenian heritage acclaimed for their work throughout the Ottoman Empire. The palace's longest-standing resident was to be the unworldly, music-loving Sultan Murad V, who having been deposed by his brother Sultan Abdülhamid II, after just ninety-three days on the throne in 1876, was to spend the next twenty-eight years effectively confined to the Çırağan Palace, making it one of the world's most sumptuous prisons. His every material need more than accommodated, Murad was to spend most of his time here contentedly reading in his vast library and tinkering about on his piano. Following his death, the palace was chosen as the home of the Ottoman Empire's first ever parliament. A building that was for so long associated with absolutist courtly excess and extravagance would therefore go on to form the backdrop to Türkiye's tentative fledgling steps towards democracy. Accordingly, it was refitted to meet the needs of the functionaries of a constitutional government in a more modern age.

The Parliament opened with some fanfare on 14 November 1909. But disaster struck just two months later when faulty electrical wiring on the palace roof caused a fire that rapidly gutted the entire building, leaving little more than its monumental stone walls standing. The Torch-Lit Palace had been torched. Among the art treasures of the palace that were lost in the blaze were several paintings by the Dutch master Rembrandt – their presence a reminder that the Bosphorus is as much a bridge as a barrier between Europe and Asia, and that the Çırağan Palace had always stood at the apex of such cross-continental currents. The French Empress Eugénie was among the Western dignitaries who toured the place in the nineteenth century and Murad, when a young prince, had visited England where he was introduced to Queen Victoria at court; the old queen taking such a shine to the Turkish prince that she attempted to broker a marriage between him and one of her granddaughters.

In ruined form, however, the palace reverted to being a pleasure garden. The remaining walls acting as the perimeter fence to a park with a sporting stadium and a

In the Ottoman era, the palace was famed for its gardens, and the hotel's discrete Secret Garden (right) more than honours that noble tradition today.

swimming pool. The former hosted football games by the Beşiktaş soccer team and the latter became a venue for swimming bouts, beauty contests and musical concerts. But in the 1980s, a plan was agreed between the visionary entrepreneur Dr Ramzi Sanbar and Türkiye's Ministry of Culture and Tourism to erect a new hotel inside the remnants of the old palace, with key elements of it fully restored – not least its exquisitely tiled hammam, the bulk of which survived the fire of 1910 – and forming part of the redevelopment.

The Çırağan Palace Kempinski Istanbul Hotel has only recently undergone a comprehensive redesign, one that has not only seen the addition of two new restaurants but also, if anything, foregrounded its Ottoman heritage in its latest furnishings and fixtures across its 317 rooms suites, bars, eateries and facilities. They pay tribute to the enchanting carpet patterns, intricate marblework and the splendour of Ottoman tent weaves of yore yet feel refined and part the twenty-first century. The hotel, nevertheless, had already clocked up over thirty years in business beside the Bosphorus under the astute stewardship of the Kempinski Hotels group. The blinking of an eye in terms of this historic locale, possibly, but impressive enough by any standards in the highly competitive luxury hospitality market. We can imagine sultans of long ago transported into our age appreciating that the Çırağan Palace Hotel remains the only hotel in Istanbul with its own registered helipad. Present day guests who opt to stay in the prestigious Sultan Suite, named in honour of the palace's progenitors, may avail themselves of a chauffeur-driven point-to-point transfer service in the hotel's classic Rolls-Royce Silver Shadow. The hotel presently offers eleven suites in the historical palace itself and each presents uniquely regal accommodations for guests regardless of their family pedigree. The hotel's award-winning Tuğra Restaurant, meanwhile, which is located on the first floor of the palace, delves deep into the imperial archives to seek out delicious recipes that excavate the best of ancient Ottoman and traditional Turkish cuisine for contemporary diners. That mix, like the hotel's enchanting combination of East and West, past and present, make it a destination worth celebrating, with coastal views that are hard to better and an august situation that is woven into the fabric of Istanbul.

◂ Top left: The historic and exquisitely tiled Hammam, decorated in the classic style, is one of the hotel's true jewels. Its interiors (top right and bottom left and right) continue in the same spirit to celebrate the best in Turkish design, ancient and modern.

▴ The palace gateway photographed in its Imperial heyday in the nineteenth century.

Çırağan Palace Kempinski is the only hotel in Istanbul with its own registered helipad.

▸ Top right: Ottoman guards on horseback. Bottom right: The Çırağan Palace Kempinski witnessed many great scenes of pageantry, here majestic horse-drawn carriages (phaetons) pull up outside the palace.

Such vehicles continue to be used across Istanbul, especially on yhe Princes' Islands, to the south-east of the historic centre in the Sea of Marmara, which is largely car-free.

Following the fire in 1909, the ruins of the palace became home to a sports stadium that hosted games by the Beşiktaş football team.

▶ The central staircase at the Çırağan Palace Kempinski in all its glory.

Top right: Dine at dusk with the Bosphorus strait before you at the hotel's award-winning Tuğra Restaurant. Top left: The once torch-lit palace beautifully illuminated at night.

Bottom right and left: The sumptuous Pasha and Sultan Suites more than live up to their regal names.

A bath fit for a king in the Sultan Suite, another perk of the room is the run of a chauffeur-driven classic Rolls-Royce Silver Shadow.

◀ Çırağan Palace Kempinski's Bellini Restaurant offers the flavours of Italy beside the Bosphorus.

▲ Standing at the watery gateway between Asia and Europe, Çırağan Palace Kempinski has a coastal location that is part and parcel of the history of Istanbul.

THE DATAI LANGKAWI

KEDAH DARUL AMAN · MALAYSIA

A high-end rainforest resort that puts nature centre stage, redefining the idea of eco-luxury for the twenty-first century.

Didier Lefort of the French architecture and interior design agency DL2A maintains, 'If you're in a place where there's nothing, it's better to make a statement; if you're in a remarkable setting, allow it to make the statement'. Lefort collaborated with the late and much-missed Australian architect Kerry Hill, who passed away in 2018, alongside the Malaysian architect Tan Sri Esa Mohamed, to design the original Datai Langkawi hotel on just such a principle back in the early 1990s. Both men, upon first visiting the site in 1989, were adamant that they should not just simply plonk the proposed hotel right on the beachfront, lovely as that might have been – and the shore of the island of Langkawi is indisputably lovely, indeed. Instead, the new hotel should be sited at a distance of three hundred metres from the Andaman Sea and some forty metres above Datai Bay. The location actually nestles within a rainforest that dates back ten million years and is a thriving, living natural habitat for monkeys and birds.

Inevitably this created headaches in terms of its master plan and in construction: there were no roads, buildings or services, so the developers were starting from scratch as it was. But the five-star resort, which finally came to extend over a sprawling sixty-five acres and was to be made up of 121 rooms, villas and suites, as well as restaurants, was one that always felt part and parcel of the forest rather than some crude intrusion into it. That feeling was reinforced by an architecture that, even though contemporary, seemed convincingly in dialogue with Malaysian vernacular traditions and the use of local and natural materials: the same *Dipterocarpus* (keruing) trees that were felled to make way for the hotel were, for instance, then used as stilts to support the structure of The Pavilion, which was to house its award-winning Thai restaurant. The hotel itself would garner a gong when it was awarded the prestigious Aga Khan Award for Architecture in 2001.

Forests may endure for millions of years but luxury hotels, alas, need updating rather more frequently, and The Datai Langkawi is no exception. In 2017, its General Manager Arnaud Girodon committed to a year-long €55 million renewal and expansion plan. But, as he put it, 'in order to find the original DNA of The Datai Langkawi' he reached out to Lefort about taking the job on, believing that his 'unrivalled knowledge of the structure, history and environment of this exceptional domain', and deep links to 'the original vision of the project' would be invaluable. Lefort readily accepted the challenge of reinvigorating the resort and reaffirming its essential essence as a landmark retreat at one with nature. As a further mark of intent, the resort also drew up a new conservation and sustainability programme, The Datai Pledge, committing it to preserving the island's wildlife and further reducing its effects on the environment.

Among the fresh buildings added to the site was a brand new and naturally ventilated Nature Centre once headed up by the hotel's former resident naturalist Irshad Mobarak and staffed by a team of ecologists and marine biologists. Built from bamboo with a thatched roof and modelled after elevated native tribal longhouses, The Nature Centre has an extensive library and guests are able to participate in hands-on scientific research and join specially curated tours of the resort's wild and sea life to enhance their understanding of biodiversity.

The hotel's Beach Club and sports and well-being facilities were also to be beefed up with a new larger pool, new terraces and pavilions and a completely new fitness centre overlooking the ocean. A set of outdoor treatment rooms was among the improvements made to the spa services. A new five-bedroom villa joined the older estate of villas and suites, all of which were completely refitted to increase their 'comfort and cosiness' yet without erasing their former rough-hewn organic appeal.

◀ The Datai Langkawi is nestled within a rainforest that dates back ten million years.

▶ The Canopy Walk enables guests to journey through the forest and experience its varied floral habitats.

◂ Top left: Enveloped by greenery, nature is omnipresent at The Datai Langkawi. Top right: Step out onto the sandy beaches and take a plunge into the inviting waters of the Andaman Sea. Bottom left: Treatments and group sessions intended to nourish body and soul, such as sound healing, yoga, meditation and pilates, are sometimes held at The Holistic Pavilion.

▴ The resort's two-bedroom villa boasts its own pool shaded by forest trees.

Nature is not some abstract idea here but ever-present, seeping into every corner of the complex in the most delightful of ways. Even when you are savouring the fine Malaysian dining offered by the prized Gulai House restaurant or sipping a signature cocktail in The Beach Club's unimpeachably smart well-stocked bar, the percussive sounds and rich aromas of the wild forest remain palpable. Indeed, a simple stroll from the main building to Datai Bay, down the Grand Staircase, the hotel's iconic 173-step walkway that was built exclusively using local materials, including chert, shale and mudstone, brings the visitor through the enchanting Butterfly Walk. Here, a habitat is provided for the roughly 535 species of butterflies that live on Langkawi. Their fragile beauty is a reminder of the preciousness that might be lost if we fail to follow the example of the likes of The Datai Langkawi; an eco resort committed to driving meaningful change for the planet and making sure its guests leave both satisfied and appreciative of the world around them.

◀ Crystal Creek (left), a pristine forest stream, where Mandi Embun is offered – a traditional forest bathing ceremony. Chef de Cuisine, Chai Chun Boon (right), puts the finishing touches to one of his acclaimed dishes in The Dining Room restaurant.

▶ At night, The Beach Club and The Beach Bar are places to unwind after a day of exercise and immersive nature experiences at the resort.

▼ The lobby of The Datai Langkawi pays tribute to timeless Malaysian vernacular traditions.

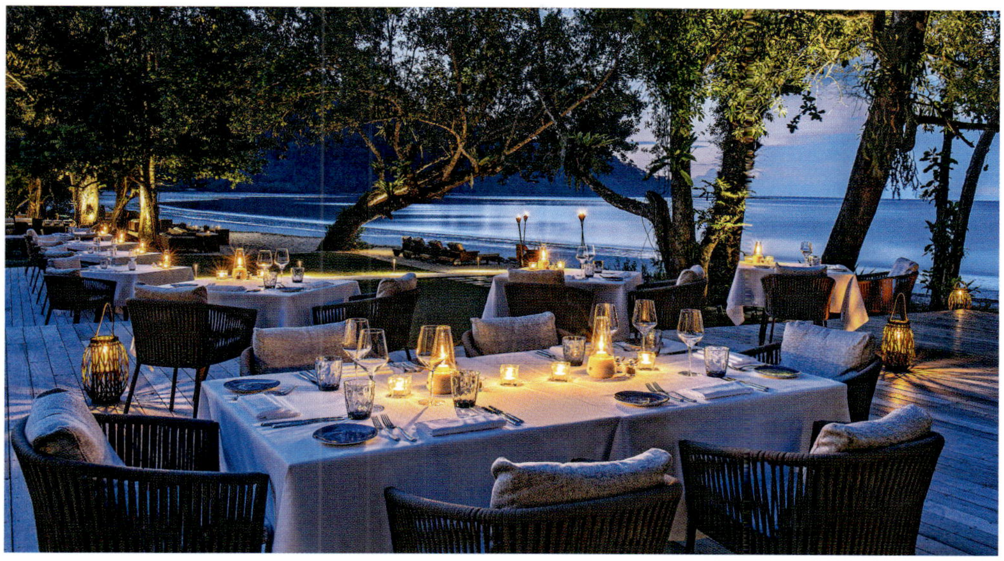

◂ Golf in the lushest of greenery at The Els Club Teluk Datai rainforest course.

▴ Top left: Interiors of the Rainforest Villa. Bottom left: The private pool of the Rainforest Pool Villa allows guests to swim under a verdant canopy.

Right: An oriental pied hornbill is one of the plethora of native birds that call this rainforest home.

◂◂ Previous double page: An overview of The Datai Langkawi at twilight.

◂ Top: The balcony of The Datai Suite opens to an enchanting forest vista and the Andaman Sea. Bottom: A view of The Els Club Teluk Datai rainforest course, which permits avid golfers a scenic game between rainforest and sea.

▸ A short distance from the hotel and in the heart of the rainforest lies the Crystal Creek, its wonderful cooling waters offering a welcome respite from the warm and humid afternoons.

SONEVA FUSHI

KUNFUNADHOO ISLAND, BAA ATOLL · MALDIVES

Soneva Fushi is an unparalleled paradise of barefoot luxury, in a sustainable ecosystem of lush jungle, pristine beaches and crystalline waters.

Hotels can be labours of love. Soneva Fushi is arguably an establishment born of even deeper passions – that of its two founders for each other, for nature and the environment, and for a very special place: the Maldives. This chain of over one thousand coral islands in the Indian Ocean is gifted with sandy beaches, lagoons and lush palm trees. The clear waters around the reefs themselves team with tropical fish and sea turtles.

But the story of the Soneva Fushi might be said to have begun in Oxford, at that British city's ancient university. It was there that Sonu Shivdasani, who was born and mostly educated in England, with spells also in Nigeria and Switzerland, was studying for a Masters in English Literature. Within this glittering citadel of academia, however, he met his Swedish wife, Eva. The two fell in love and married. Not long afterwards, they visited the Maldives and were enamoured with it to such an extent that in 1990 they wound up leasing an island there with the idea of creating a resort hotel was born.

Luxury was vitally important to them but so too was the environment. Soneva Fushi – the first part of its name containing the couple's forenames melded together – was accordingly envisioned as a beach spa that could compete with the world's best but without costing the earth itself dearly. To their minds, going barefoot on the golden sands did not necessarily mean skimping on the finer things. It just required imaginative thinking about doing them as sustainably as possible. And Soneva Fushi, which opened for business in 1995, has been widely acclaimed ever since for providing a blueprint for how such a resort might look after their guests and the planet at the same time.

For instance, in 2008, Soneva Fushi pioneered the banning of all branded bottled water from the resort and began filtering, mineralizing and bottling its own water on site. In turn, investing the subsequent financial savings made in supporting clean water projects around the world. It then developed its own carbon calculator to measure Soneva's direct and indirect CO_2 emissions, as well as external emissions such as guest flights, as the resort can only really be reached by seaplane or speedboat. With these figures at its fingertips, though, it was able to introduce a mandatory carbon levy on all guest stays to offset that damage, with proceeds going towards the not-for-profit Soneva Foundation. So far the Soneva Foundation has funded the planting of thousands of trees in Thailand, paid for the construction of a 1.5-megawatt windmill in India and financed the distribution of hundreds of energy-efficient cookstoves to rural communities in Myanmar and Darfur.

Today, the resort has its own carbon-neutral upcycling studio, where it turns waste aluminium cans and plastic bottles into useful objects and artworks, and the Eco Centro Waste-to-Wealth, a further workshop that transforms other trash into treasure.

It also prides itself on running the world's first fully sustainable surfing programme with wave chasers at the resort able to enjoy their sport with eco-friendly and recycled equipment during the high surfing season between May and September.

There is, it should be stressed, nothing hair-shirted about the resort. Its architecture may take its cues from nature and be constructed of locally sourced wood and materials; but primitive, it is not. The scenic seventy-one villas that comprise the resort's suites all come, as might only be expected at this juncture, with air-conditioning, Wi-Fi, televisions and Bose sound systems. More compellingly, though, each villa has its own stretch of private beach or waterfront and alongside decks with sun loungers and daybeds there are sunken bathing pools and showers to allow you to soak in (quite literally), every facet of your surroundings.

Wellness and communing with nature in all its facets are really the whole point here. You can embark on

◀ Soneva Fushi is a resort that reaches right out into the pellucid waters of the Indian Ocean.

▶ This single-bedroom villa comes with its own water slide.

This nine-bedroom villa complex offers spacious communal lounging areas and a central pool in which to cool off.

KUNFUNADHOO ISLAND, BAA ATOLL · MALDIVES

meandering jungle trails or go swimming and snorkelling with the manta rays in nearby Hanifaru Bay. Take a cruise out to watch the dolphins cavorting in the sea at sunset or drink in the heavens above at the Observatory with helpful commentary from Soneva Fushi's resident astronomers and visiting expert stargazers. There are yoga sessions in the Turtle Beach Champa, a glass-walled sala with the ocean and the greenery of the forest serving as its backdrop. And the wonders of marine life below the sea are yours to explore, too, with an underwater diving session led by one of the resort's multi-lingual PADI instructors.

For younger guests, there is also the Soneva Academy where children and teens can learn about the natural world with tailor-made courses on the night sky, mosquitoes and the aquatic treasures of the deep. More carefree fun is another option at The Den, one of the largest children's zones in the Maldives.

Eating and drinking well is no less important, and visiting Michelin-starred chefs in its various eateries serve up everything from classic grills and barbecues with freshly caught seafood to modern style sashimi, torched wagyu beef, black cod and other Japanese favourites with a contemporary twist. Vegan and vegetarian options are sourced from Soneva Fushi's organic garden. Located in the heart of Kunfunadhoo Island, it supplies all of the resort's kitchens with a variety of fresh fruits, vegetables, herbs and mushrooms to ensure that all of its tables are replenished with the most ecological of locally grown produce.

◂ Top: The Fresh in the Garden restaurant offers farm-to-table dining in a forest setting. Bottom: This four-bedroom villa offers a poolside lounger perfect for lazing in the sun.

▴ The sun is celebrated, too, in this villa's decorative detailing.

◂ Top: Staffed by resident astronomers, the Observatory is an out of this world facility for guests to improve their appreciation of the heavens above. Bottom: An aerial view of the resort in all its glory.

▴ Soneva Fushi's organic garden supplies all of its kitchens with a wealth of fresh fruits and vegetables.

◀ Top: The reef around Soneva Fushi teams with tropical fish and turtles. Middle: The water reserve villas provide oceanside luxury living. Bottom: Take a cruise to watch the dolphins and become acquainted with the marine life of the Maldives.

▶ Enjoy a private dinner on the sand illuminated by candle light and the evening sky.

Eat out over the water in Out of the Blue, Soneva Fushi's sensational Pan-Asian restaurant.

ATLANTIS THE ROYAL

DUBAI · UNITED ARAB EMIRATES

An experience that will completely redefine the perspective of luxury. This is the place where something incredible happens at every moment of your stay.

Atlantis The Royal began with a competition brief that challenged its would-be architects to create 'the most memorable building in the city'. That the city in question was Dubai, already home to the Burj Khalifa, the tallest building in the world, and the Royal's sibling-neighbour, the no-less eye-catching Atlantis The Palm, is indicative of the leap in architectural imagination demanded. The winning design by Kohn Pedersen Fox Associates, the American architects behind the seventy-three-storey super skyscraper One Vanderbilt in New York, supposedly started out as a scribble on a napkin. Eight years later, the finished hotel would be opened with a Moët & Chandon-soaked three-day extravaganza where Beyoncé sang in public for the first time in half a decade. The amount of her undisclosed fee was almost as big a topic of conversation as the building itself. *Almost* anyway, for the 795-room Atlantis The Royal is an awesome – in the true meaning of the word – proposition. An almost mind-bending building by any standards, it is an incredible addition to The Palm Jumeirah skyline.

Standing some forty-three storeys high and running to nearly half a kilometre in length, the Atlantis The Royal is an architectural marvel composed of six staggered and interlocking concrete and glass tower blocks that are connected by a ninety-metre-long sky bridge. If roped to each other, the blocks each have their own separate identities. With raked, almost ziggurat-esque storeys interspersed throughout with indoor spaces that seek to replicate the feel of shaded Arab courtyards and gleaming desert oasis pools, the hotel presents orchid-rich gardens in the sky and bathing in pellucid waters at extraordinary heights. The region's resources also shape some of the offerings in the hotel's spa, with treatments featuring oud perfumes, dates, Dubai desert sand and Persian Gulf sea salt among the multitude of therapies as well as wellbeing and beauty sessions.

As it happens, only three of the six towers, (Sunrise, Sunset and Sunlight) actually form part of the hotel complex, the others operate as blocks of private flats. But it is a measure of the sheer scale of the place that its hotel guest accommodation still runs to 760 rooms, including 623 Standard Rooms, 98 Suites and 6 Signature Penthouses. Its forty-four signature suites and penthouses all come with terraces, landscaped greenery and their own private infinity pools. Running parallel to the central sky bridge, however, is the hotel's main swimming pool. The 295-foot long Skypool makes swimming an aerial adventure by placing an entire beach some twenty-two floors above ground. The Skypool also forms part of Club 22, an open-air entertainment venue with a swim-up bar, a stage and DJ booth to keep the party pumping but also private plunge pools and VIP cabanas to hire for more intimate gatherings.

Overall there are more than ninety pools of one kind or another across the whole hotel. Indeed, water is a theme that permeates every aspect of the Atlantis The Royal's design and interior decor, from the pattern of the carpets with undulating swirls of blue and turquoise to rolling tidal folds of the soft furnishings. One quoted source of inspiration, however, is not the nearby ocean but the water wells that sustained and guided the nomadic Bedouin on their epic journeys across the Arabian Desert. This is brought vividly to life by Droplets, the colossal eleven-and-a-half-metre-high stainless-steel sculpture that is the centrepiece of the Atlantis The Royal's main lobby and a shimmering three-dimensional representation of the first cool drop of rain to fall on bone-dry desert sands. More astonishing still are the central Deluge lifts, a pair of three-storey-high cylindrical glass elevators that are sheathed in rippling water that cascades down their sides into glistening pools below. Whisking guests up and down from the lobby to the mezzanine restaurants on the third floor, the Deluge lifts offer an

◂ **The Skyblaze fountain, this dazzling water feature depicts the play between fire and water that underscores the hotel's design.**

▸ **The cool, serene lobby of the Royal Mansion.**

utterly unique means to move through the building; the experience is akin to being conveyed by waterfall. Some 3,500 gallons of endlessly recycled water in a state of constant circulation is needed to keep it flowing. Also in the lobby are three vast aquariums, illuminated by state of art LED lighting that causes the ripples from the movements of the more than 7,200 marine creatures they contain to paint dappled patterns across the room.

Wait, however, until you see the hotel's jellyfish aquarium. The largest in the world, its ingeniously fashioned tank, which is nearly seven metres deep, contains over four thousand specially reared glow-in-the-dark moon jellyfish. It provides a backdrop, suitably reminiscent of Jules Verne, to Resonance, the concept bar devised by Heston Blumenthal, the British chef acclaimed for bringing scientific rigour and a sense of mischief to his multisensory menus. At Resonance, the drinks come lab tested as molecular cocktails, guaranteed to cause the most pleasing of chemical reactions, top of the bill.

Blumenthal also operates the Dinner restaurant at the hotel, this Michelin-starred eatery proffering playful reinterpretations of such historic British dishes as tipsy cake and spit-roasted pineapple pudding for your gastronomic delight. The hotel has seventeen restaurants in all, Blumenthal just one of a number of starry big names at the Atlantis The Royal with their own dedicated culinary outlets. The celebrated Spanish-American chef José Andrés provides paella and other Iberian classics at Jaleo. The best Greek food outside of the Mediterranean is yours in Estiatorio Milos, the Dubai branch of Costas Spiliadis's internationally admired taverna. While Nobu delivers Nobu by the Beach, bringing their famed Japanese-Peruvian fusion food poolside. Gastronomy, meanwhile, the first-floor artisanal buffet has the joyful bustle of a souk. Seating close to one thousand, with some six hundred inside its spacious refectory and three hundred more on an open-air terrace with panoramic views, its seventeen-strong kitchen stations put all the finest flavours of the world within easy reach. It is a prime spot for breakfast and great for grazing, as well as gazing at your fellow diners, Palm Jumeirah and the Dubai Marina beyond. Gastronomy is as glorious a foodie melting pot as one might hope for from a hotel that employs staff from 107 different nations alone.

◂ Top feft: The ornate trumpet lamps and the loungers of the sky-high Cloud 22 poolside area, pictured at midnight with the space bathed in soothing light. Bottom left: Soak up the sun and swim some laps at the family-friendly Royal Pool.

▴ The stunning Sky Pool Villa's terrace at sunset.

◀ The lobby, with its impressive aquarium and water features make a memorable first impression.

▶ Top right: Flowers are another feature of the lobby, as these epic displays amply demonstrate. Bottom right: The stainless-steel jumping water spheres bring a touch of wonder to the Royal Galleria, the lower ground floor retail avenue.

The north terrace of the Royal Mansion, with the stars and twinkling lights of the Dubai skyline lighting up the night.

▸ Top right: The sitting room of the Sky Terrace suite is a room with a near unequalled view. Bottom right: The Royal Mansion Bar is one of the best places to toast the sunset in style.

◂ The pineapple rotisserie in Heston Blumenthal's Michelin-starred Dinner restaurant.

▸ Top right: The Ultra Lounge in Ling Ling, the hotel's spirited Pan-Asian bar-restaurant and party venue. Bottom right: The terrace view of Heston's Dinner, the restaurant that serves up a cutting-edge take on classic British cuisine.

Sample unforgettable views of the Palm, an archipelago of artificial islands on the Persian Gulf, from the terrace of the Royal Mansion.

DUBAI · UNITED ARAB EMIRATES

CAPELLA SYDNEY

SYDNEY · AUSTRALIA

For generations, the Department of Education building stood quietly, its golden sandstone façade forming an unassuming backdrop to the rhythm of the city. It has since become a destination in its own right as Australia's most original new hotel in decades.

DEPARTMENT OF EDUCATION
24-30
CAPELLA

Footsteps away from Sydney's most iconic landmarks, Capella Sydney is part and parcel of the city yet an oasis of calm in the midst of the bustle of the financial district.

Although a new hotel, and one which only opened its doors in 2023, the Capella Sydney is a thoroughly modern enterprise that might be said to have heritage on its side. For the hotel is not only located on ancient lands which the Gadigal Aboriginal people of the Eora Nation occupied for thousands of years before colonization, but it is also housed some of Sydney's most notable former government buildings in the heart of the city's financial district. On the face of it, being given the chance to bunk up in what was once the headquarters of the New South Wales Department of Public Instruction (later renamed the Department of Education) or its adjoined neighbour, the one-time offices of the Department of Agriculture, might not sound all that appealing. Yet both of these buildings were expressions of early twentieth-century civic pride at its most noble and intended with every sandstone block to exemplify the ambitions of what was then the newly unified Australian nation when it came to feeding its citizens' minds and bodies.

The building of the Department of Education, designed in the style of Edwardian Baroque or Federation Free Classical, and inspired by the likes of the Renaissance-era Palazzo Farnese in Rome, was the work of the Scottish-born Australian architect George McRae in 1912. McRae was a native of Edinburgh and, having emigrated to Sydney at the age of twenty-seven in 1884, rose to become the Government Architect of New South Wales, a position he held until shortly before his death in 1923. He would equip Sydney with some of its liveliest institutional buildings, among them the Queen Victoria Building in George Street, a grandly domed municipal market building in the Romanesque style, and the Parcels Post Office on Railway Square, another Federation Free Classical edifice, itself converted since into a hotel, along with the pseudo-Mogul elephant house in the city's Taronga Zoo – a structure purpose-built to accommodate the Asian variety of these animals, hence its Orientalist bent.

A southern wing to house the offices and research laboratories of the Department of Agriculture was added to the Education building in 1930. Though its creators, the firm of John Reid and Son were able to avail themselves of newer methods of steel-framed construction, and the new wing was clad rather than built in sandstone, it was a complementary building, one that gracefully extended McRae's original schema while possessing its own distinct qualities. Five years later, cementing the newer building's place in the district, the adjacent public square was named Farrer Place, in honour of William Farrer, the Australian agronomist who had developed the disease-resistant 'Federation' strain of wheat at the turn of the twentieth century. If that connection remains etched into the landscape and written on maps, the Department of Agriculture eventually left the building for new premises in the late 1970s, after which the Department of Education assumed control of both wings until they too finally departed in 2018.

It was then that Pontiac Land Group, who had been awarded the lease for these buildings along with another government office across the street, the Department of Lands building, the stately Victorian former headquarters of the survey office and land registry of New South Wales designed by the Colonial Architect James Barnet in 1870, began the process of converting them into a hotel. Their collaborators on this project was Make Architects, who were responsible for the exclusive The Oasis at Golden Sands resort on Malta.

The Department of Lands Building is expected to join the completed complex in 2026 with additional luxury retail and restaurant offerings, but the result so far is already a five star hotel with 192 guest rooms, three bars and restaurants, function rooms and event spaces that more than holds its own against more august

With cityscape views and deep-soaking bathtubs, the hotel's Skyline Rooms are airy, with an abundance of natural light.

competition, perhaps in part because of the sensitive ways in which period details and historical finds have been preserved and, indeed, foregrounded in the site's new incarnation.

While the original building has been extended by four floors, the newer levels were set back to ensure that the original line of the building was retained. A particular gain from the refit was the reinstatement of the old internal garden courtyard on the ground floor. Canopied by a glass roof and rich with vegetation and dazzling contemporary artworks, including *Meadow*, a robotic light installation by Amsterdam's Studio Drift, it serves as the main Aperture lounge area and airy central atrium of the hotel. Elsewhere, the original directory boards of the old Agricultural Building have been kept in situ, but instead of holding the details of the departments and employees, their elegant brass frames contain works by the Waanyi artist Judy Watson. These, in turn, are a response to the ingenious and colonial history of the area – such layering of the past and present is a recurring theme in the hotel's decor and design.

In the process of the refit, many archaeological discoveries were made and artefacts dating from the late eighteenth and nineteenth centuries unearthed. Some of these objects have been incorporated into a display on the wall of the main lounge, called The Living Room, that is oriented around an enlarged reproduction of a map of the British colony made by the convict Francis Fowkes in 1788. One of the major finds during the reconstruction was the cistern of the stone fountain that once stood on the corner of Bent and O'Connell Streets; a Sydney landmark for nearly a hundred years, it was eventually removed in 1905 to make way for new tramlines. Such was the price of progress back then. Today questions of sustainability rather than mere sentiment help to drive global conversions about what to do with buildings and facilities that have outlived their former functions – Capella Sydney providing an exemplary case in point.

One of the most inventive reimaginings was the installation of a spa and twenty-metre swimming pool into an area on the sixth floor that had historically served as a public gallery for art exhibitions of school children. The reflective surface of the pool, dappled in sunlight from the vintage skylights, offers an enchanting visual spectacle of its own, in a place once given over to looking. Redundant timber floorboards from across the two buildings were used to create the spa treatment rooms, while heritage-listed light wells allow natural daylight into these spaces, the old once more folding into the new, something further emphasized by the range of treatments in the spa that are respectfully modelled on ancient indigenous rituals and that use specially sourced Australian ingredients and sacred stones.

Capella Sydney's culinary offering is equally and proudly Australian, too, with even its main restaurant Brasserie 1930, offering a 'uniquely Australian' take on the classic brasserie experience and masterminded by Brent Savage and Nick Hildebrandt, head chef and sommelier, respectively, and the team behind the award-winning Bentley Restaurant + Bar in Sydney's CBD, the central business district. The hotel's daily ritual, Echoes of Eternity, meanwhile, is a cold brew coffee liqueur whose name salutes the legendary local character Arthur Stace, a church caretaker who chalked the word 'Eternity' in yellow around Sydney for more than thirty years.

◂ The hotel's swimming pool, a spectacle in itself, is located in a former gallery for the art of school children..

▴ Well-appointed modern, spacious rooms offer a window onto the past and present.

▸ Aperture, the venue in the reimagined Farrer Place foyer, occupies the magical, light-filled space at the centre of Capella Sydney.

◀ The hotel's heritage-listed walls tell their own story, as do the meticulously curated artworks and furnishings that fill its reimagined interiors.

The classic brasserie dining experience has been given a modern edge.

▲ While now four storeys taller, the new floors do not disturb the line of the original building, merely adding an additional and fetching crown to the structure.

Les Clefs d'Or

Les Clefs d'Or (which literally translates from French as 'The Golden Keys') is the name of the professional association of international hotel concierges, dedicated to meeting the needs of their guests and constantly striving to set new professional standards in hospitality.

The figure of the concierge first emerged in the late nineteenth century when grand hotels sprang up to accommodate the burgeoning number of affluent tourists and business travellers liberated to venture further and faster thanks to new continent-spanning railway lines and ocean-shrinking steamships. If the hotel porter or doorman became the focal point of many hotels, the separate role of the concierge, often seated behind the front desk, was specifically created to assist the guests with their itineraries and needs in unfamiliar cities and grew to become a vital cog in the machinery of any well-run establishment.

In the late 1920s, a group of concierges from hotels in Paris (and one in Algeria, then a French colony) and headed by Pierre Quentin, the concierge of the then only recently opened Hôtel Ambassador in boulevard Haussmann, began discussing the idea of forming a club to pool ideas and experiences. On 26 October 1929, Quentin convened a dinner for these likeminded concierges at the restaurant Noël Peters in the Passage des Princes just across from his hotel, which ultimately led to Les Clefs d'Or being formally ratified a month later and Quentin elected as its first president. In 1936, Les Clefs d'Or set up home in premises at 12 rue Cambon in Paris, which remains the association's headquarters to this day.

Pierre Quentin's presidency of Les Clefs d'Or was followed by François Dechaume, who was elected in 1932 and remained at this position until the war. He was among the eleven founding members. Sadly, there was no activity of Les Clefs d'Or during the war as all hotels, especially in Paris, were occupied by Germans forces. But just as the United Nations and the European Common Market were both born of the never-again spirit of post-war reconciliation and international cooperation, so Dechaume's successor, Ferdinand Gillet, was to put Les Clefs d'Or on the path to becoming the global organization it is today. The 25 April 1952 is held as a historic date for the association, for it was on that day that its first international congress opened at The Carlton Hotel in Cannes. Attended by representatives from France, Italy, Switzerland, Germany, Great Britain and Ireland, and with Belgium and Denmark as observers and Spain as a guest, it marked the association's reinvention as a body committed to connecting concierges across the continent, and by the 1970s, it had already grown well beyond Europe. In 1998, the name, Union Internationale des Concierges d'Hôtels 'Les Clefs d'Or' (UICH), was officially adopted to reflect its expansive world-wide reach.

Today, the association is an elite and globally connected fraternity with approximately 3,200 members working in over eighty counties and in 530 destinations in every corner of the world. Its members may be easily recognized by the crossed golden keys emblem worn on their jacket lapels. But entry to this guild must be earned. Those who aspire to join must have several years' experience as a hotel concierge and pass a series of tests to prove beyond doubt that they possess the ability to deliver the highest quality of service.

Its current President, Randy Santos, embodies the ethos of Les Clefs d'Or in the twenty-first century. Beginning his career as a bell boy in the Philippines in the early 1990s, he advanced his career as hotel concierge in Dubai before moving to the Fairmont in Doha, where he was appointed Chief Concierge and spearheaded the founding of Les Clefs d'Or chapters in Qatar and the UAE. After serving as its First International Vice-President, he was elected to the top job in 2023, becoming the first President of Les Clefs d'Or working in the Middle East.

Santos believes passionately that it is the responsibility of a Clefs d'Or concierge to 'make the impossible possible', and that it is beholden on the organization's members to always 'do more than expected'. The overriding motto of UCIH is, as he points out, 'In service through friendship'. That motto, he maintains, requires that his members provide a 'customized and excellent service' for guests on 'a daily basis' and the mutually supportive nature of the fraternity, in turn, helps them achieve this.

Les Clefs d'Or has nearly a hundred years of history behind it now. When it was founded, the aeroplane and multi-funnelled ocean liner were the novel thing and jazz and women in trousers quite shocking. Looking to the future and what the next thirty years might bring, Santos is adamant that 'the enduring demands of the human connections and personalized experiences will ensure that the concierge role continues'. And AI, he not only concedes 'is coming', but it must also be 'embraced' as a 'useful tool'. One that he feels will probably 'make things faster in terms of admin', thereby freeing the concierge to be even more attentive to guests on a personal basis. Ultimately, he argues, its use and how that might alter the role of the concierge will be driven by the demands of the guests. But the concierge, and Les Clefs d'Or, he is sure, will still be with us in the centuries to come.

PICTURE CREDITS

OPENING IMAGES (PAGES 6–15)

- Çırağan Palace Kempinski, Istanbul, Sultan's Dinner
- Hotel Sacher, Vienna, view from the hotel onto the Vienna State Opera
- The Datai Langkawi, Kedah Darul Aman, The Pavilion
- Atlantis the Royal, Dubai, House of Dessert
- The Dolder Grand, Zurich, staircase
- Hotel Vier Jahreszeiten, Hamburg, reception
- Taj Mahal Palace, Mumbai, Ayurveda
- The Pierre NY, a Taj Hotel, lobby
- Soneva Fushi, Maldives, organic gardens
- Le Bristol Paris, Paris, wine cellar

INTRODUCTION (PAGES 16–19)

- Le Bristol Paris, Paris, Salle Épicure
- Hotel Sacher, Vienna, entrance

FRONTISPICE

©Freepik

HOTEL SACHER

©Hotel Sacher: pp. 7, 19, 21–35; Madame d'Ora/Arthur Benda 27.

HOTEL VIER JAHRESZEITEN

©Hotel Vier Jahreszeiten: pp. 42, 43 (4), 45; ©Hotel Vier Jahreszeiten–Matthias Plander 37; ©Hotel Vier Jahreszeiten–Max Arens 38, 39, 44 bottom right, 48 middle and bottom, 49; ©Hotel Vier Jahreszeiten–Guido Leifhelm 41, 44 top, 50/51; ©Hotel Vier Jahreszeiten–René Supper 11, 44 bottom left, 48 top; ©Hotel Vier Jahreszeiten–Christof Haake 46/47.

THE DOLDER GRAND

©thedoldergrand: pp. 10, 53–67. © VG Bild-Kunst, Bonn 2025 for Juan Munoz, Conversation Piece, 1993, p. 63.

THE TAJ MAHAL PALACE

©Taj Mahal Palace: pp. 12, 69–83.

MANDARIN ORIENTAL HYDE PARK, LONDON

©Mandarin Oriental Hyde Park, London: pp. 85, 86/87, 89 (3), 90 (3), 91, 92 (2), 93 top, 94 (2), 95; picture alliance/empics/PA 93 bottom left; picture alliance/dpa/ Kay Nietfeld 93 bottom right.

LE BRISTOL PARIS

©Le Bristol Paris: pp. 107; Benoît Linero 15; Maki Manoukian 17, 98, 105; Romain Réglade 97, 99, 102 top; Claire Cocano 101, 103, 104, 106 top, 109 top left, 111; Eric Denisette 102 bottom; Gérard Uféras 106 bottom; Franck Juery 108; Vincent Leroux 109 bottom left, 110 bottom left and right; Franck Bohbot 109 right; Julia Krikorian 110 top left and right.

THE PENINSULA HONG KONG

©The Peninsula Hong Kong: pp. 113–123.

THE PIERRE NY

©The Pierre NY, a Taj Hotel: pp. 130, 131, 133 (2), 136 (5), 137 bottom, 138/139; Andrew Werner 13; Yuxi Liu 125, 126/127, 129, 132, 137 top; Ron Galella 134, 135 top right; Getty Images 135 top left and middle; Robert Levin 135 top middle.

VILLA LA MASSA

©Villa La Massa: pp. 141–151.

ROYAL PALM BEACHCOMBER LUXURY

©Beachcomber Resorts & Hotels: pp. 153, 157; Jean-Bernard Adoue 154/155, 159, 160/161; Anne-Emmanuelle Thion 158; Eric Cuvillier 162 (3); Mélissa Pierre 163.

ÇIRAĞAN PALACE KEMPINSKI

©Çırağan Palace Kempinski: pp. 6, 165–179.

THE DATAI LANGKAWI

©The Datai Langkawi: pp. 181, 182/183, 186 (3), 187, 188 (2), 189 (2), 190, 191 bottom left, 192/193, 194 (2); Eric Martin 8, 185; Marion Payr 191 top left and right, 195.

SONEVA FUSHI

©Soneva Fushi: pp. 203, 204 top; Matt Porteous 14, 205; Stevie Mann 197, 206 middle, 208/209; Sandro Bruecklmeier 199, 202 top and bottom; Richard Waite 200/201, 206 bottom, 207; Julia Neeson 204 bottom; Fabio Giungarelli 206 top.

ATLANTIS THE ROYAL

©Atlantis the Royal, Brandon Barré: pp. 9, 211–224.

CAPELLA SYDNEY

©Capella Sydney, Timothy Kaye: pp. 227–237.

LES CLEFS D'OR

©Les Clefs d'Or: p. 239.

COLOPHON

A member of Penguin Random House Verlagsgruppe GmbH
Neumarkter Strasse 28 · 81673 Munich

First edition

produktsicherheit@penguinrandomhouse.de
(The above information is mandatory information according to GPSR and should be used for all queries relating to the safety of our books.)

Library of Congress Control Number is available; a CIP catalogue record for this book is available from the British Library.

Editorial Direction: Claudia Schönecker
Project Management: Andrea Bartelt-Gering
Text: Travis Elborough
Copyediting: José Enrique Macián y Fijałkowski
Cover Design and Layout: Sofarobotnik, Augsburg & Munich
Production Management: Luisa Klose
Separations: Reproline Mediateam, Unterföhring
Printing and Binding: TBB a.s., Banská Bystrica

MIX
Paper | Supporting responsible forestry
FSC® C022120

Penguin Random House Verlagsgruppe FSC® N001967

Printed in Slovakia
ISBN 978-3-7913-8047-6
www.prestel.com